LAS VEGAS
The Delaplaine
2020 Long Weekend Guide

Andrew Delaplaine

NO BUSINESS HAS PAID A SINGLE PENNY OR GIVEN _ANYTHING_ TO BE INCLUDED IN THIS BOOK.

Senior Editors - *Renee & Sophie Delaplaine*
Senior Writer - **James Cubby**

Gramercy Park Press
New York - London - Paris

Please submit corrections, additions or comments to
andrewdelaplaine@mac.com

TABLE OF CONTENTS

Chapter 1
FIRST THINGS FIRST

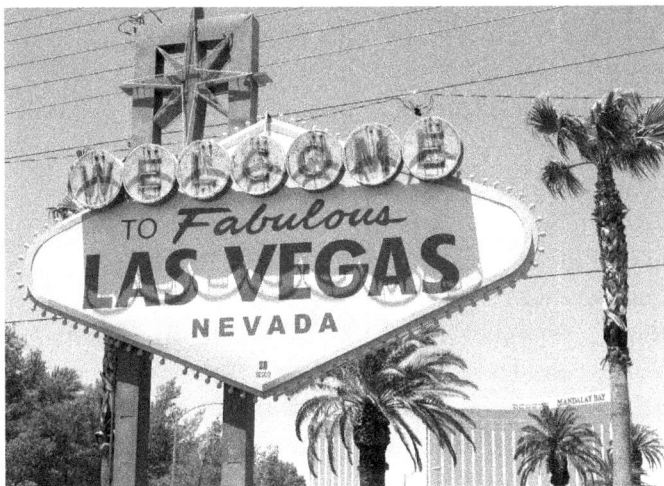

WHY LAS VEGAS?

If you've never been to Vegas before, you're in for a treat. One thing I can guarantee you is that you will not leave Vegas without strong feelings about it—one way or the other.

I know people who absolutely love it, people who travel here once a month to get their gambling "fix." Even when they could go to any number of other places to gamble, they choose Vegas. It has an allure that is beyond comprehension. When you get here, you'll understand what I mean. These people are just nuts about Vegas, can't get enough.

On the other hand, I know people who can't stand the place, people who say it represents all the vulgarity extant in American life, all rolled up into one town in the middle of an inhospitable desert in what used to be the wilds of southern Nevada. Once upon a time, it was every man's description of a true No Man's Land. Go figure. Just shows what happens when you mix the Mafia with a little bit of water. (OK, a lot of water!)

I remember when George W. Bush was decrying al Qaeda after the 9/11 attacks. One of his favorite mantras was: "They're trying to destroy our way of life." A friend of mine who had just returned from Vegas (and loathed every minute of the experience), turned to me and said, "Well, if they can take out Vegas, maybe that wouldn't be such a bad thing." Eek!

One thing about Vegas: there are no halfhearted responses to this town.

Even if you aren't a gambler, hate flashy shows and don't even drink: you owe it to yourself to visit this place. See what the Tawdry Girl is all about. Find out what all the ruckus is about.

Vegas is one of the most unique towns not just in America, but the world, and you have to see it to believe it.

BUGSY & THE BEGINNING

Maybe you've seen the movie Bugsy starring Warren Beatty. Then again, maybe you haven't. It's well worth it just to get an idea of what this dump looked like in the '40s when he stumbled upon it. They really did recreate the vast emptiness of the town. And you can understand why all the East Coast mobsters thought he was nuts to want to go out to Nevada and build a casino in a desert.

That was in the mid-1940s when Bugsy opened the famous Flamingo. One thing you can say about him: he was right.

Still, gambling got there before Bugsy (or he wouldn't have shown up to begin with). Legislation was passed in 1931 to permit gambling. The population had been scant (like ZERO) before 1928, but the place became a little boomtown after workers started pouring in to build the nearby Hoover Dam in 1928. So as soon as the guys building the dam got their paychecks, small casinos opened to relieve them of their earnings. (And you think it's hard to beat the house today?)

Well, the rest is history. The Mob moved in and made millions by giving the customer what he wanted.

Big hotel conglomerates have moved in and largely squeezed out the old Mafia crowd that really got Vegas started and stabilized and generated so much of Vegas' history, but there are still some organized crime connections in the town (according to rumor).

THE LAY OF THE LAND

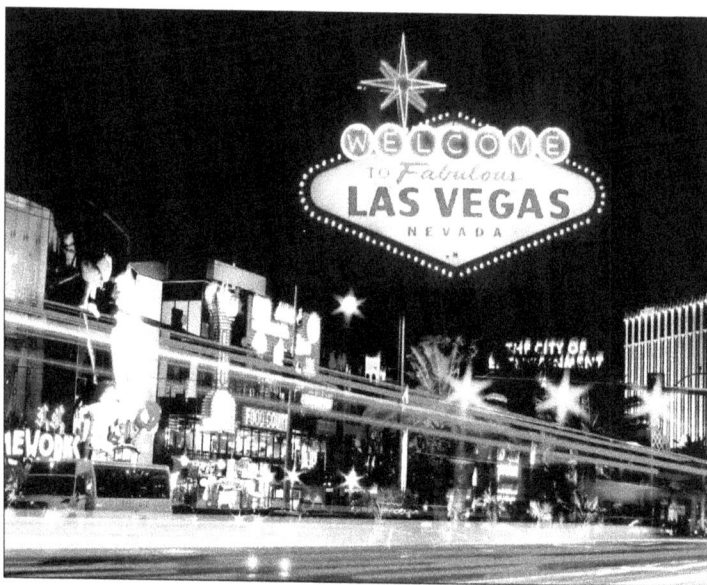

Las Vegas couldn't be a simpler town to navigate. It's laid out like the smallest towns in America.

The Main Street runs north to south. All streets with numbers similarly run north-to-south.
"The Strip," that world-famous highway to hell (or heaven, depending on your view) is also called Las Vegas Boulevard South. It starts just south of Downtown. Here is where you'll find the big casino hotels ranged along the road, lined up like the Sirens ready to seduce Odysseus onto the deadly rocks of Fate. (Well, maybe not that dramatic. All they want is your money.)
Finding something in Vegas is quite easy. Everything is "on The Strip," or it's "off The Strip," or it's "downtown."

TRANSPORTATION & TIPS FOR GETTING AROUND

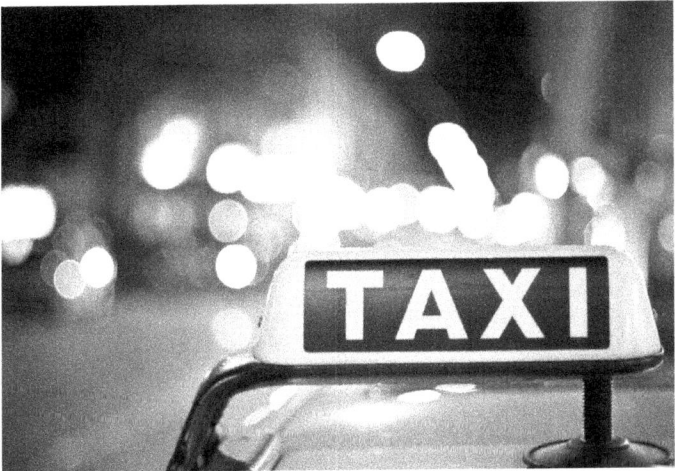

TAXIS / UBER / LYFT

Taxis are ubiquitous, along with Uber & Lyft. That's the good news. It's best to get a cab wherever you are (hotel, casino, etc.) because there they will be plentiful. It's illegal for a taxi to stop on The Strip to pick you up if you try to hail them. If you want to hail a cab on The Strip, position yourself at the corner of a cross street. That way, the cabbie can turn off The Strip and pick you up with no hassle.

Dispatchers at hotels ought to be tipped a dollar or two. Normal tipping applies to cabbies, 15% to 20%. They do regulate taxis in Vegas, so if you feel like you've been handled poorly, take down the cabbie's number and report your complaint to the Nevada Taxi Cab Authority.

LIMOS

Always a good option for larger parties. You'll see them lined up everywhere. You can negotiate directly with the driver.

THE SHUTTLE

There's a frequent shuttle that runs up and down The Strip. Traffic in Vegas is either good or it's bad. It always seems to vary from one extreme to another. Very often you'll be in bumper-to-bumper traffic.

WALKING

Since everything seems so close, walking makes a lot of sense. I'll let you decide for yourself how hot is too hot to walk. As with everything else in Vegas, the weather is a matter of extremes. Hot or cold. The only one of the elements you usually don't have to worry about is rain.

THE MONORAIL – 702-699-8200

This runs along the east side of The Strip, with stops at the Convention Center and the bigger hotels. But it does not go to the airport and it doesn't go Downtown, so it's only of marginal use. (I wonder if the taxicab lobby had anything to do with the Monorail not going to the airport, thus saving visitors untold millions a year that they could then throw away at casinos.)

BUSES

Always an attractive alternative to walking. They run along The Strip and also Downtown. If the bus lines are really long, walk a block east of The Strip to Paradise Rd., or a block west to MLK Blvd. and use the buses on those streets as they run parallel to The Strip and can be much faster.

SCOOTERS

Still another option, if you're up for it. **Sun Scooter Rental,** 702-275-2379, offers free delivery to most hotels.

RENTING A CAR

I never do it unless I'm planning to leave town on a side trip somewhere. It costs more in taxi fares, but I find it less hassle. The casinos have free parking if you do have a car. And valet parking if you want to pay for convenience.

I-15

This interstate road is parallel to The Strip and is used by locals to avoid The Strip entirely. Just get off at the exit nearest your destination and find parking.

EAST-WEST TRAVEL

Just as you'd use I-15 to travel rapidly from north to south, you'd use the Desert Inn Rd., specially built to get people from east to west.

SPECIFIC INFORMATION DURING YOUR VISIT

This site, www.visitlasvegas.com, has lots of current information. Also, www.lasvegastourism.com.

DELAPLAINE'S
TOP 8

A purely subjective list, as any list like this has to be. I'm not going to tell you to walk down The Strip to look at the neon. Or to eat at a mammoth hotel buffet. Or to visit several casinos to take in the different design themes. You'll do these things merely in the course of being here. But there are a few things you ought to do before you leave.

(No particular order)
1. Go to the Fremont Street Experience downtown. (See Attractions.) This is Glitter Gulch at its finest. The old neon signs for the city's past have a very

special enchantment that brings to mind many ideas about Vegas, most of them subconscious.

2. Go to a Cirque de Soleil show, even if you've been to one of the touring versions. The touring versions, while truly eye-popping, do not rise to the world of the spectacular until they are experienced in a room dedicated to that particular show's special needs. Here, you get the whole experience.

3. Go to a big show. You have to go to a big show. The bigger the better. See who's playing during your trip and go see a star. (See the nightlife chapter.)

4. Go to a dive bar frequented by locals. See what it's like in Vegas when you're not a tourist. For an even more interesting look, go to a locals' gay bar.

5. Go hotel lobby bar hopping. Have one or two drinks in five or six over-the-top hotels and stroll around looking at what money can buy. (Remember, I said money, not taste.)

6. Have a truly gourmet meal. Vegas for its whole existence has been about quantity (the groan-inducing buffets at all the hotels are testaments to this lasting legacy that will never be eradicated), and only recently has quality entered the equation with the arrival of world-famous chefs. It's become a blood sport for the top toques of the culinary world to outdo each other in Vegas. You are the direct beneficiary of these efforts. My personal choice would be L'Atelier de Joël Robuchon in the MGM Grand. The chef has a

more expensive and more traditionally "fine dining" restaurant in the Joël Robuchon at the Mansion, also in the MGM Grand, but the countertop setting in the diner-like L'Atelier I find more interesting because you get to interact with the people on the other side of the counter. If food is art, at these two places, you're entering a world-class museum.

7. Go to the Grand Canyon and Hoover Dam. I know, they aren't even in Vegas, but still. To get a feeling for the actual environment Las Vegas is in the middle of, these two places can't be beat.

8. Visit five wedding chapels. Did you know that over 200,000 people actually get married in Vegas every year? That's right. And they can choose from 60 different wedding chapels. These affairs keep the Elvis impersonators in business. I've listed some of the chapels. (Most hotels have chapels as well, but they aren't as interesting as the stand-alone versions.)

Chapter 2
LODGING

LAS VEGAS HOTELS

The sumptuousness of Vegas hotels has long been
legendary. And whenever you encounter a friend
who's a big shot in Las Vegas (and you always do),
they brag on and on about how they're treated like

royalty at Caesars Palace or the Bellagio, or wherever they hang their hat when they're in town.

I get sick of hearing it (okay, jealous might be a better word): how they never pay for their lavish suites. They never pay for their meals. How they get flown out to Vegas. I even know a big spender in Miami who gets a visit from a hotel man in Vegas who takes her to dinner once a year at Joe's Stone Crab!

Finally, I realized that the reason they don't pay for anything in the room is because of what they do spend downstairs in the casino!

Hey, the house always wins. One way or another.

There are three sections to consider staying in Las Vegas: The Strip, Off Strip or Downtown.

HOTEL DISCOUNTS

There's a company called Tix4Tonight that sells discount tickets to almost every show, often at half-price the box office price. **www.tix4tonight.com**. I wouldn't be surprised to find out they sell more tickets to the shows than the hotels do themselves. I've never used anybody but these people. And even if others are paying, I do them a favor and give them this web site. However, the reason I mention them here is that they also offer steep discounts on some big hotels. Well worth looking into before booking.

THE STRIP

ARIA RESORT & CASINO
3730 Las Vegas Blvd S., Las Vegas: 702-590-7111
www.aria.com
This is one big property: 4,000 rooms that went up in
2009. At the heart of the Las Vegas Strip, ARIA is
located in CityCenter, a collection of upscale
shopping, dining and art venues that takes up almost
70 acres. ARIA's dramatic architecture houses an

1800-seat theater and 2-level spa. Dubai World is a partner here, and it shows because they have certainly brought along a touch of class (and not the phony kind so dramatically on display everywhere else in Vegas). You know all that smoke choking you in the other casinos? Not here. They have an ingenious system that sucks it out right in front of the smoker sitting at a slot machine. The smoke never gets a chance to circulate.

Another thing you'll notice here is Art with a capital "A." They've spent a fortune on it. In the lobby, there's an 80-foot-long sculpture called "Silver River" by Maya Lin. But you'll see plenty of art wherever you look. Don't rush by without giving it some time.

The rooms here are ultra modern. By the bed you'll find a console with push-button controls. You might think you need a master's degree to figure it out, but with a little practice, it's easy enough. You can control everything that happens in your room (well, except maybe in bed) from this console.

There's a huge Elvis Store here with some really good souvenirs. (Curiously, there's not a lot of this kind of Elvis stuff in Vegas, and you'd think there'd be an Elvis Store on every corner.)

The restaurants here are amazing: they've put together some of the world's most acclaimed chefs and restaurant people: from Jean-Georges Vongerichten to Sirio Maccioni, Michael Mina, Julian

Serrano, Michelin 3-star winner Chef Masayoshi
Takayama, who serves up his Japanese culinary
works of art at BARMASA. There's also **Shawn
McClain,** a James Beard Award winner whose food
you can taste at **Sage**.

BALLY'S LAS VEGAS
3645 Las Vegas Blvd S., Las Vegas: 877-603-4390
www.ballyslasvegas.com
Hotel rises 26 floors above The Strip. Next door is
The Paris Las Vegas Resort. Just a few minutes to the
Sands Expo Center.

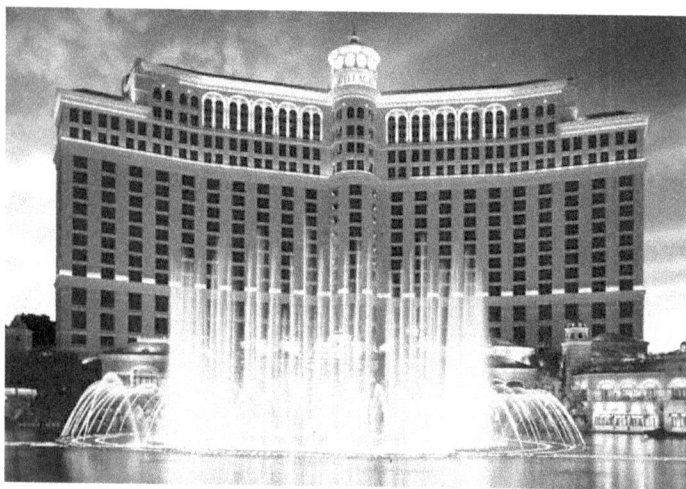

BELLAGIO
3600 Las Vegas Blvd S., Las Vegas: 888-987-6667
www.bellagio.com
The Big Mama of them all. I just had to stay here
when they first opened. Still do, sometimes. On 122
acres. Of course, you know all about the famous
fountains set to music.

CAESARS PALACE

3570 Las Vegas Blvd S., Las Vegas: 866-227-5938
www.caesarspalace.com
You'd think this place would get tired someday, but
NO. It's still a thrill to enter the place. They have a
new hotel tower, the Octavius (688 new rooms),
which brings their room count up to a staggering
3,960 rooms and suites. The Octavius has its own
valet entrance, a separate lobby and rooms a bit
larger, like 550 square feet. The latest in-room
technology.

CIRCUS CIRCUS HOTEL & CASINO

2880 Las Vegas Blvd S., Las Vegas: 800-634-3450
www.circuscircus.com
Casino, yes, but it has a family-friendly tilt. Circus
Tower with big top tent roof. They actually boast of
having the world's biggest permanent circus on
premises and when you see it, you'll be amazed.

When you gamble here, don't be distracted by the acrobats twirling around above you while they hang from the ceiling. (Go figure.)

Camping: Next door to Circus Circus is a KOA-operated campground, Circusland RV Park with 400 spaces offering full utilities. The campground has its own little world: there are pools, Jacuzzis, a dog park, food store, arcade for the kids, playgrounds, etc.

THE COSMOPOLITAN OF LAS VEGAS

3708 Las Vegas Blvd. S., Las Vegas: 702-698-7000
www.cosmopolitanlasvegas.com
Rises 52 floors so you get spectacular views.

DELANO

Mandalay Bay
3940 S Las Vegas Blvd, Las Vegas, 702-632-7888
www.delanolasvegas.com
NEIGHBORHOOD: The Strip

Set in a 43-story tower on the Mandalay Resort complex at the southern end of the Strip, this recently renovated hotel features 1,117 elegant suite-style rooms. Named after famed Delano Hotel in South Beach, this beautiful hotel features art installations and gorgeous décor throughout. Quite a bit more "elegant" than the flashier hotels Vegas is known for. (Of course, one could argue that if you wanted elegant, what the hell are you doing in Vegas to begin with, right? You want elegant instead of outrageous, go to Paris.) Amenities include: complimentary Wi-Fi, flat-screen TVs, and iPod stations. Guests can use the pool complex at the Mandalay Bay, on-site spa and fitness center. **Franklin Bar** located off the lobby. Dog-friendly rooms available.

ENCORE AT WYNN LAS VEGAS
3121 Las Vegas Blvd S., Las Vegas: 702-770-7171
www.wynnlasvegas.com
Though it's part of the Wynn, it's NOT a part. It's next door. This place has superior views of the city. It's got a totally different vibe than the Wynn. The Encore Tower Suites are just the best in town.

EXCALIBUR HOTEL & CASINO
3850 Las Vegas Blvd S., Las Vegas: 702-597-7777
http://www.excalibur.com
Camelot is the theme here. Note the castle gates. Some call this place "the Realm," and it really is a world unto itself. Medieval moats, castle turrets, a drawbridge. You get the idea. The place just goes on and on and on and you wonder where the designers come up with some of this stuff. It's all as fake as a blow-up sex doll, but what the hell. It's Vegas. Family friendly. Good prices. Lots of stuff for kids.

FLAMINGO LAS VEGAS
3555 Las Vegas Blvd S., Las Vegas: 702-733-3111
http://www.flamingolasvegas.com
28-story casino hotel on 30-acre site featuring Wildlife Habitat, 15 acres of pools, lagoons, streams and waterfalls. On The Strip.

FOUR SEASONS HOTEL LAS VEGAS
3960 Las Vegas Blvd S., Las Vegas: 702-632-5000
https://www.fourseasons.com/lasvegas/
Sophisticated non-gaming hotel situated at the south
end of The Strip, within the Mandalay Bay Resort &
Casino Complex. This is a very nice change from the
typical Vegas experience. One of my favorite places
to stop.

HARD ROCK HOTEL AND CASINO
4455 Paradise Rd., Las Vegas: 702-693-5000
http://www.hardrockhotel.com
Eleven-story hotel adjacent to Hard Rock Cafe &
featuring rock 'n roll memorabilia throughout.

HARRAH'S LAS VEGAS
3475 Las Vegas Blvd S., Las Vegas: 800-214-9110
www.harrahslasvegas.com

Popular resort comprising a carnival-themed hotel and a 35 story tower; located at the Carnival Court shopping area.

THE LINQ HOTEL & CASINO
3535 Las Vegas Blvd S., Las Vegas: 800-634-6441
www.caesars.com/linq
Contemporary tower hotel with ornate, traditional Asian style, center of Strip - Connected by monorail to Las Vegas Conv Center.

MANDALAY BAY
3950 Las Vegas Blvd S., Las Vegas: 877-632-7700
http://www.mandalaybay.com
All-suite hotel connecting to Mandalay Bay Resort; contemporary brown, bone and beige decor, plasma TVs, marble/granite bathrooms.

MANDALAY BAY RESORT & CASINO
3950 Las Vegas Blvd S., Las Vegas: 877-632-7700
http://www.mandalaybay.com
This one goes up 43 floors. Has an 11-acre tropical water park, extensive foliage. On the south end of The Strip, it's next to the Mandalay Bay Convention Center.

MGM GRAND
3799 Las Vegas Blvd. S., Las Vegas: 877-880-0880
http://www.mgmgrand.com
There are many places in Vegas where the term "city within city" applies. This is most certainly one of them. If you've never been to Vegas before, you'll find just checking into this place to be a daunting affair. They even have these big screens to let you know what's going on in the complex (rather like the airport). Though the place has been through several renovations, there still are signs of the original theme, the Golden Age of Hollywood, with big photos of the great stars of the past.

All 3,570 rooms and 642 suites in the main tower came off a $180 million refurbishing in 2012, with upgrades to the furniture and a change to a warmer color palette.

The Signature is a non-casino all-suite hotel next to the MGM Grand that offers quite a bit less chaos from the tumult in the main tower and the West Wing (more upscale lodgings).

Those monitors can come in handy, since so much does go on here. You'll find Joël Robuchon's two eateries here, **L'Atelier de Joël Robuchon** as well as the more plush "fine dining" restaurant in the **Joël Robuchon at the Mansion.** Stepping down a notch with a "Bam!" is Emeril's New Orleans Fish House.

You can't call the swimming pool a pool, it's a pool "area" encompassing almost seven acres of space. Lush landscaping surrounds the five pools, a river and a cabana club, the Wet Republic.
The Grand Spa is one of the largest in town, approaching everything with a Zen calmness completely alien to Vegas you'll reencounter once you leave the subdued confines of the Spa.
Entertainment. Not only does the MGM have Cirque de Soleil's KÁ here (see chapter with Cirque shows), but a nightclub called Studio 54 (see Nightlife), the Lion Habitat (see Attractions), an adult topless extravaganza called Crazy Horse Paris (see nightlife). How can you not fall in love with a place that has Joël Robuchon under the same roof as a bunch of strippers? Welcome to America!

NEW YORK-NEW YORK HOTEL & CASINO
3790 Las Vegas Blvd S., Las Vegas: 702-740-6969
http://www.nynyhotelcasino.com
Replicates (well…) a dozen iconic New York buildings.

NOBU HOTEL AT CAESARS PALACE
Caesars Palace Las Vegas Hotel & Casino
3570 Las Vegas Boulevard South, Las Vegas, 800-727-4923
www.nobucaesarspalace.com
NEIGHBORHOOD: The Strip
The world's first Nobu Hotel is a luxury, celebrity-favorite 181-room 5-star hotel. This hotel features 6 outdoor pools, a casino and a restaurant. Guests have personalized concierge assistant. Amenities include: Priority access to Nobu restaurant, complimentary toiletries, flat-screen TVs, MP3 player docking, and complimentary Wi-Fi. Walking distance to Fashion Show Mall.

THE PALAZZO RESORT HOTEL CASINO
3325 Las Vegas Blvd. S., Las Vegas: 702-607-7777
http://www.palazzo.com
Of the top Las Vegas hotels, The Palazzo sets new standards with Five-Diamond luxury throughout this premier all-suite Las Vegas Casino.

PARIS LAS VEGAS
3655 Las Vegas Blvd S., Las Vegas: 877-796-2096
http://www.parislv.com
What they do at New York-New York, here they do to Paris. This may be the only time you ever get to go to the Paris Opera and wear shorts at the same time.

PLANET HOLLYWOOD RESORT & CASINO
3667 Las Vegas Blvd S, Las Vegas: 866-919-7472
http://www.planethollywood.com
This is not your hometown Planet Hollywood.

SOUTH POINT HOTEL, CASINO & SPA

9777 Las Vegas Blvd S., Las Vegas: 702-796-7111
http://www.southpointcasino.com
60 acre, Mediterranean style resort, casino and equestrian center in Southwest Las Vegas - 8 minutes to heart of The Strip.

STRATOSPHERE CASINO HOTEL & TOWER

2000 Las Vegas Blvd S., Las Vegas: 800-998-6937
http://www.stratospherehotel.com
Entertainment Hotel Complex & Casino featuring a new 24-story Hotel Tower & 1149 ft Observation Tower.

THE HOTEL AT MANDALAY BAY RESORT AND CASINO

3950 Las Vegas Blvd. S., Las Vegas: 877-632-7800
http://mandalaybay.com
THE Hotel at Mandalay Bay ushers in a new model of understated luxury, affording guests a haven of sophistication and service on par with the best boutique hotels in the world. Its elegantly appointed suites and stylish lobby areas set a tone of confident discretion, while its carefully tailored roster of amenities provides an unparalleled atmosphere for attending to both business and pleasure. Something different: a non-casino hotel.

TREASURE ISLAND

3300 Las Vegas Blvd S., Las Vegas: 800-944-7444
http://www.treasureisland.com

The only hotel you always expect Johnny Depp to walk out of. It seems like Disney ought to own the place, since TI (that's what it's called in these parts, TI) copied the whole Pirates theme from Disney. They've changed a lot of this, however, and the pirate show is for the most part history. In lieu of the "pirate show," they have guys toying with "sirens." The Cirque de Soleil's Mystère is located here, along with the usual hotel buffet. A famous L.A. deli, Canter's Deli, is also here, and it's definitely one of the two best delis in Vegas. An excellent spa is on the premises.

THE VENETIAN RESORT HOTEL CASINO
3355 Las Vegas Blvd. S., Las Vegas: 702-414-1000
http://www.venetian.com
The Venetian sets the standard for luxury in Las Vegas throughout this legendary all-suite Las Vegas resort, with careful attention paid to every detail of their lavish suites. With suites up to 1500 square feet, featuring a sunken living room, marble bathroom, two LCD flat-screen TVs, and so much more. Experience the comforts of this elegant home away from home and you may never want to leave your room, though there's plenty to drag you out to shop, dine and play.

WALDORF ASTORIA LAS VEGAS
3752 Las Vegas Blvd. S., Las Vegas: 702-590 8888
www.waldorfastorialasvegas.com
Formerly the Mandarin Oriental, Waldorf Astoria Las Vegas is a sophisticated luxury hotel and residences prominently located at the entrance of CityCenter, a magnificent urban resort destination at the heart of the

Las Vegas Strip. Awarded the esteemed AAA Five Diamond Award rating and the coveted Forbes Five-Star award for their Spa, they offer fine-dining, a relaxing Spa, spectacular accommodations and legendary service all steps away from some of the city's most renown casinos, shopping and entertainment.

WYNN LAS VEGAS
3131 Las Vegas Blvd S., Las Vegas: 702-770-7000
www.wynnlasvegas.com
Wynn's masterpiece, a 50-story hotel with a 170 foot mountain and 5 waterfalls. Close to the Convention Center.

OFF STRIP

ALEXIS PARK RESORT HOTEL
375 E Harmon Ave., Las Vegas: 702-796-3300
http://www.alexispark.com
It's all designed in a Mediterranean style. Lots of water, lush vegetation. Two blocks from The Strip.

COURTYARD LAS VEGAS CONVENTION CENTER
3275 Paradise Rd., Las Vegas: 702-791-3600
http://www.marriott.com
This Las Vegas convention hotel features a new lobby with inviting, flexible spaces in which to work or relax with free Wi-Fi throughout and easy access to the latest news, weather and airport conditions via their GoBoard. The highlight of the new lobby experience is The Bistro. Family-friendly.

FAIRFIELD INN LAS VEGAS AIRPORT
3850 South Paradise Rd., Las Vegas: 702-791-0899

http://www.marriott.com

This Las Vegas Airport hotel is in downtown Las Vegas just 2 blocks from The Strip. Hop on the hotel's free shuttle to head to the Las Vegas Airport, The Strip, or the nearby Convention Center. The recently renovated Marriott Fairfield Inn hotel provides a comfortable, quiet escape at a substantial value. Luxurious bedding, cable TV with HBO and free high-speed internet. Free hot breakfast, modern hotel fitness center, pool.

WESTGATE LAS VEGAS RESORT & CASINO

3000 Paradise Rd., Las Vegas: 702-732-5111
http://www.thelvh.com
Next door to Las Vegas Convention Center, 1 block off The Strip.

LA QUINTA INN & SUITES

3970 Paradise Rd., Las Vegas: 702-796-9000
http://www.lq.com
The La Quinta Inn & Suites Las Vegas Airport North Convention Center (Whew! What a name!) is two miles north of McCarran Airport and 1.3 miles from The Strip; 3/4 mile from the Convention Center, with over one million square feet of exhibition and convention space on one level and the adjacent Sands Expo Center.

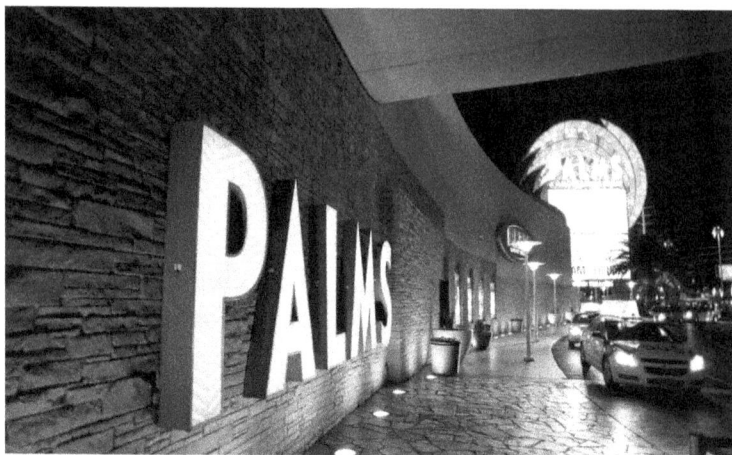

PALMS CASINO RESORT
4321 W Flamingo Rd., Las Vegas: 702-942-7777
www.palms.com
This 40-floor property sits on 32 acres, but it's a mile
from The Strip.

RIO ALL SUITE HOTEL & CASINO
3700 W Flamingo Rd., Las Vegas: 866-746-7671
http://www.riolasvegas.com
Two towers, 20 and 41 floors. A little over a half mile
to The Strip. They have a shuttle.

SILVER SEVENS CASINO & HOTEL
4100 Paradise Rd., Las Vegas: 702-733-7000
www.silversevenscasino.com
Two miles from The Strip, you'll find this nice resort
that is designed in an Italian Renaissance style.

VDARA HOTEL & SPA

2600 W. Harmon Avenue, Las Vegas: 702-590-2111
http://www.vdara.com
MGM Resorts owns this resort at CityCenter. Non-gaming, non-smoking, eco-friendly, all-suite is located between ARIA and Bellagio on the Strip. Access all the gaming, dining, shopping, and nightlife CityCenter has to offer. AAA Four Diamond Award, a rooftop pool & lounge, spa & salon.

THE WESTIN CASUARINA LAS VEGAS HOTEL, CASINO & SPA

160 East Flamingo Rd., Las Vegas: 702-836-5900
http://www.westinvegas.com
Stay here if you want a calm sanctuary amidst the bustle of Las Vegas. The action and excitement of The Strip is just a block away—and a quiet retreat whenever you need some peace.

DOWNTOWN

EL CORTEZ HOTEL & CASINO
600 E Fremont St., Las Vegas: 702-385-5200
http://www.elcortezhotelcasino.com
Casino Hotel walking distance from Fremont Street
Experience.

FOUR QUEENS HOTEL & CASINO
202 Fremont St., Las Vegas: 702-385-4011
http://www.fourqueens.com
Right in the middle of the Fremont Street Experience.

GOLDEN NUGGET HOTEL & CASINO
129 E Fremont, Las Vegas: 702-385-7111
http://www.goldennugget.com
This famous joint deserves a go-see even if you're not
staying down here.
The Fremont Street Experience is outside.

MOTEL 6
195 E Tropicana Avenue, Las Vegas: 702-798-0728
http://www.motel6.com
This is the largest Motel 6 and is located across the
street from the MGM Grand. Many casinos are within
walking distance. Downtown's Fremont Street
Experience is a short trip away. WiFi available in all
rooms for a modest fee.

Chapter 3
RESTAURANTS

THE STRIP

ANDREA'S AT ENCORE
Wynn Las Vegas
3131 Las Vegas Blvd S, Las Vegas, 702-770-5340
www.wynnlasvegas.com/Dining/FineDining/Andreas
CUISINE: Asian Fusion
DRINKS: Full bar
SERVING: Dinner
PRICE RANGE: $$$
NEIGHBORHOOD: The Strip

Sleek, luxurious eatery offering great views of Club Surrender. Menu features seafood, table-sharing dishes, sushi and favorites like the Wagyu Beef and Lobster dish. Great place for a special occasion. Nice wine selection.

AUREOLE
LAS VEGAS, NV

AUREOLE
3950 Las Vegas Blvd S., Las Vegas: 702-632-7401
mandalaybay.com
CUISINE: American
DRINKS: Full Bar
SERVING: Dinner
Prestigious Chef Charlie Palmer has finally brought his famous New York restaurant to Vegas. This sleek, dramatic restaurant, located in the Mandalay Bay Hotel, offers a stunning setting in which to enjoy Palmer's equally stunning American cuisine. The

seasonal menu offers prix fixe and tasting options, showcasing the best produce, meat, and fish available. Here dining is art, and the four-story, climate-controlled, wine tower housing over 9,000 bottles, is a masterpiece in its own right. Be sure to catch the "wine angels," black-clad wine stewardesses who are hoisted up and down the tower to retrieve bottles each evening. (Only in Vegas would they even think of such a stunt.) $$$$

BARDOT BRASSERIE
Aria
3730 S Las Vegas Blvd, Las Vegas, 702-590-7757
www.aria.com
CUISINE: French
DRINKS: Full bar
SERVING: Dinner
PRICE RANGE: $$$
NEIGHBORHOOD: The Strip
Michael Mina's French brasserie features a great dining experience with an atmosphere that's designed to "take you back to Paris of the 1920s." Menu favorites include: Black truffle fries, and Mussels Marinières. A favorite for weekend Brunch with specialty dishes like their incredible French toast and Croque Madame.

BAZAAR MEAT BY JOSÉ ANDRÉS
SLS Las Vegas
2535 S Las Vegas Blvd, Las Vegas, 702-761-7610
www.slslasvegas,com/bazaar-meat
CUISINE: Steakhouse/Spanish/Tapas-Small Plates
DRINKS: Full bar

SERVING: Dinner
PRICE RANGE: $$$$
NEIGHBORHOOD: The Strip
Philippe Starck–designed steakhouse featuring Chef José Andrés creative menu celebrating meat. Grand restaurant with five different food stations preparing different types of food. Try the suckling pig. They make "cotton candy" using foie gras. Sick, isn't it? Until you taste it. Great tasting menu.

BUDDY V'S RISTORANTE
Venetian Hotel
Grand Canal Shoppes
3327 S Las Vegas Blvd, Las Vegas, 702-607-2355
www.buddyvlasvegas.com
CUISINE: Italian/American (Traditional)
DRINKS: Full bar
SERVING: Lunch & Dinner
PRICE RANGE: $$
NEIGHBORHOOD: The Strip
Upscale eatery serving classic Italian fare. Menu favorites include the Chicken Parm and Spaghetti Central with Meatballs. Large portions perfect for sharing. Nice wine selection.

BURGER BAR
3930 Las Vegas Blvd S., Las Vegas: 702-632-9364
www.burgerbarlv.com/
CUISINE: Burgers
DRINKS: Full Bar
SERVING: Lunch/Dinner
This burger joint is from internationally acclaimed Chef Hubert Keller, and reflects his keen eye for

detail, quality, and flavor. We all crave the simpler pleasures in life: a thick, juicy burger with all the fixings and a decadently sweet drink to follow, and the Burger Bar delivers. The refined diner in us demands quality above all else; options like the Country Natural and American Kobe Beef burgers are excellence in a bun. From a frothy milkshake to a heady beer, finding satisfaction here is easy. $

CAPITAL GRILLE

3200 Las Vegas Blvd. S., Las Vegas: 702-932-6631
www.thecapitalgrille.com
CUISINE: Steakhouse
DRINKS: Full Bar
SERVING: Lunch/Dinner
Superior steak, seafood and a fine wine selection are typical features of Capital Grille. Rich woods and seductive lighting that combine to create everyone's image of what a steakhouse ought to look like. That's the only problem with it – there's no surprise here. In Vegas you want to be surprised. Yes, they have quality aged meat and fresh seafood flown in daily from both coasts. Still, you know, there are Capital Grilles all over the country. Skip this and go to any number of other places that offer similarly great food but in a setting you won't find at home. $$$

CHINA POBLANO

The Cosmopolitan of Las Vegas
3708 S Las Vegas Blvd, Las Vegas, 702-698-7900
www.chinapoblano.com
CUISINE: Chinese/Mexican
DRINKS: Full bar

SERVING: Lunch & Dinner
PRICE RANGE: $$
NEIGHBORHOOD: The Strip
A project of famed Jose Andres, here is a unique combination of Chinese and Mexican fare but realize the two cuisines are not served together. You choose either one, you can have both. Yes, you can order a taco and duck tongue at the same time. Steamed BBQ pork buns are the best. Watch the cooks make the tortillas and dumplings by hand. There's a fried rice with 20 veggies in it. The rou jia mo sandwich comes on a flatbread that's simply divine. Creative fusion cocktails, something you almost never see in Asian eateries. But then, this place is unique in all the world. Never saw anything quite like it. (And it works!)

COSTA DI MARE
3131 Las Vegas Blvd. S., Las Vegas: 702-770-3305
http://www.wynnlasvegas.com/Restaurants

CUISINE: Italian, Seafood
DRINKS: Full Bar
SERVING: Dinner
The live seafood (over 40 varieties offered) flown in daily from the Mediterranean is show-stopping. That alone, combined with startlingly authentic ingredients such as Sicilian olive oil and imported porcini mushrooms, makes this place special. The gorgeous al fresco dining space overlooks a dreamy lagoon, and a whimsical, two-level indoor dining room is gorgeous. Understated, but still decadent, the AAA-Four-Diamond-rated restaurant is the closest diners will get to the shores of Italy on this side of The Strip. $$$$

CRAFTSTEAK
MGM Grand
3799 S Las Vegas Blvd, Las Vegas, 702-891-7318
www.mgmgrand.com
CUISINE: Steakhouse/Modern American
DRINKS: Full bar
SERVING: Lunch & Dinner
PRICE RANGE: $$$$
NEIGHBORHOOD: Eastside
Fine-dining experience with a menu from James Beard Award Winning chef Tom Colicchio. Menu features steaks, seafood, and typical American fare made from locally sourced small farms and the world's top ranchers. A truly vast collection of Scotches (not to mention bourbons as well). The heavy dark woods and plush atmosphere combined with carefully selected and exceptionally prepared steaks create a superior dining experience your

steakhouse back home can't come close to. (It's
places like this—where everything is perfect—that
sets Vegas aside.)

CUT BY WOLFGANG PUCK
The Grand Canal Shoppes
3325 S Las Vegas Blvd, Las Vegas, 702-607-6300
https://wolfgangpuck.com/dining/cut-las-vegas/
CUISINE: Steakhouse
DRINKS: Full bar
SERVING: Dinner
PRICE RANGE: $$$$
NEIGHBORHOOD: The Strip
Great place for steak lovers with excellent choices
like the Nebraska rib eye and Nebraska filet mignon.
If you have room left, order the baked Alaska.
Reservations recommended.

DICK'S LAST RESORT
3850 Las Vegas Blvd S., Las Vegas: 702-597-7991
http://www.excalibur.com/restaurants/dicks_last_reso
rt.aspx
CUISINE: American
DRINKS: Full Bar
SERVING: Lunch/Dinner
The Las Vegas location of Dick's Last Resort, in the
Excalibur, is famous for being one of the rowdiest
restaurants because the staff here is trained to be
"insensitive" to their guests. Or, just plain rude. The
menu at Dick's offers great barbecue and American
cuisine, drawing influences from Texas. A wide
selection of barbecued meats, seafood, and Dick's
signature Buckets O'Grub. (It's better than it sounds,

trust me.) The messy menu items at Dick's Last Resort mirror the laidback and crazy atmosphere of the place. $$

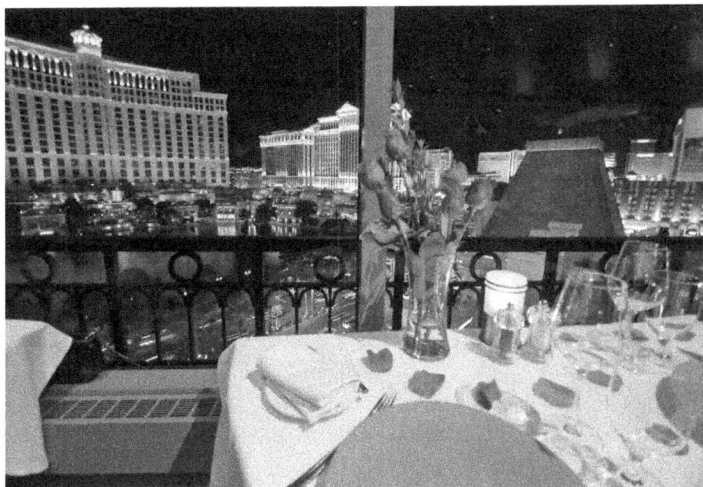

EIFFEL TOWER
3655 Las Vegas Blvd. S., Las Vegas: 702-948-6937
http://www.eiffeltowerrestaurant.com
CUISINE: French, Steakhouse
DRINKS: Full Bar
SERVING: Lunch/Dinner
Located on the eleventh floor of the Paris Las Vegas Eiffel Tower replica, the restaurant boasts a remarkable view of the Las Vegas Strip and the fountain show at the Bellagio. The glass elevator is the pathway to a romantic spot that is destined to create a love affair with the city of Las Vegas with its panoramic views of the city. The creative and dramatic menu updated by world-renowned Chef J.

Joho brings light to conventional French cuisine as he provides his unique interpretation of menu items that represent the merging of originality with tradition. $$$$

EMERIL'S NEW ORLEANS FISH HOUSE
3799 Las Vegas Blvd. S., Las Vegas: 702-891-7374
www.emerilsrestaurants.com
CUISINE: American, Seafood
DRINKS: Full Bar
SERVING: Lunch/Dinner
Emeril. He's an institution, a household name. He's made cooking fun and easy for everyone, and has restaurants in New Orleans, Las Vegas, Orlando, Atlanta, as well as Gulfport. He owns the trademark Emeril's, as well as famed Delmonico's. Here at the MGM since 1995, the place was renovated in 2009. The restaurant is sexy, and the food is exciting. Their wine list is more than fifty pages (and way overpriced). $$$

ESTIATORIO MILOS
The Cosmopolitan
3708 S Las Vegas Blvd, Las Vegas, 702-698-7930
www.cosmopolitanlasvegas.com
CUISINE: Greek
DRINKS: Full bar
SERVING: Lunch & Dinner
PRICE RANGE: $$$$
NEIGHBORHOOD: The Strip
This terrace eatery offers Greek & Mediterranean-style dishes with a focus on seafood. Great fixed-price lunch menu. Dinner more an elegant affair. This place offers a top-notch dining experience offering the best of everything. Great selection of Greek wines.

FOUNDATION ROOM
3950 Las Vegas Blvd., Las Vegas: 702-632–7631
www.houseofblues.com
CUISINE: Asian, Indian
DRINKS: Full Bar
SERVING: Dinner
Have you ever wondered what's on the roof of Mandalay Bay, and why people crowd outside in the summer time? Or have you pondered where all the beautifully dressed ultra chic people emerge from en masse, descending upon the House of Blues? Welcome to the Foundation Room. Originally a 'members only' secret, accessible only via a private elevator in Mandalay Bay, the Foundation Room began last summer opening up to the public and is now open to locals on Monday and Thursday nights.

Distinguished, with tasteful vintage décor, the food mirrors the appointments inside, combining Asian and Indian influences with European flair and some luxurious versions of American comfort classics. $$$

GIADA
The Cromwell
3595 S Las Vegas Blvd, Las Vegas, 855-442-3271
www.caesars.com
CUISINE: Italian
DRINKS: Full bar
SERVING: Breakfast, Lunch & Dinner
PRICE RANGE: $$$
NEIGHBORHOOD: The Strip
Celebrity chef Giada De Laurentiis' first restaurant here in the desert is a celebration of Italian cuisine, to the point that the whole experience is very homey and friendly. A beautiful welcoming restaurant featuring a dining room, lounge, outdoor patio with breathtaking views of the Bellagio fountains and Caesars Palace. Menu features Italian dishes with a California twist like: Chicken cacciatore, Marsala herb chicken meatballs and Vegetable Bolognese rigatoni. There's even a pizza made using carbonara. (Who'd ever have thought of that?) Creative cocktails. Great choice for brunch. When you get the tasting menu, they'll give you the recipes to take home with you.

GOLDEN STEER STEAKHOUSE
308 W Sahara Ave, Las Vegas, 702-384-4470
www.goldensteerlasvegas.com
CUISINE: Steakhouse
DRINKS: Full bar

SERVING: Dinner
PRICE RANGE: $$$
NEIGHBORHOOD: The Strip
This is Vegas' longest-running steakhouse and you almost feel like you've been transported back to the "Old Las Vegas" when waiters wore tuxedos. Menu features "The Best Steaks on Earth" as well as seafood and Italian specialties. The only restaurant in Las Vegas that serves Bananas Foster tableside as a flambé.

GRAND BUFFET
3799 Las Vegas Blvd S., Las Vegas: 702-891-7433
www.mgmgrand.com/restaurants/mgm-grand-buffet.aspx
CUISINE: Buffet
DRINKS: Full Bar
SERVING: Breakfast/Lunch/Dinner
MGM's Grand Buffet captures the decadence and glamour of classic Hollywood. Breakfast stations run the gamut from the Heart-Healthy Station with fruit compotes and yogurts (which I know you're going to walk right past without so much as a disdainful glance) to the more-like-it honey baked ham, smoked salmon, and made-to-order omelettes. Lunch offers similar variety like lighter Seasonal Salads, a festive Quesadilla of the Day option, and a tempting Dessert Station that promises "something for everyone." Spend the weekend with the Grand Buffet team and you're in for a treat: dinners offer a staggering display of delicacies like Alaskan Crab Legs, Roast Prime Rib, and Grilled Marinated Beef Kabobs sure to satiate appetites of all kinds and (especially) sizes. $$

GUY SAVOY

Caesars Palace
3570 S Las Vegas Blvd, Las Vegas, 702-731-7286
www.caesars.com/caesars-palace/restaurants/guy-savoy
CUISINE: French
DRINKS: Full bar
SERVING: Dinner; closed Mon & Tues
PRICE RANGE: $$$$
NEIGHBORHOOD: The Strip
This French eatery truly offers a top-notch dining experience. Designed to reflect the menu of the Paris restaurant featuring many of the original signature dishes. Everything here is the best and is prepared perfectly. Impressive wine list. Reservations recommended.

GUY FIERI'S VEGAS KITCHEN & BAR

The LINQ Las Vegas Resort & Casino
3535 S Las Vegas Blvd, Paradise, 702-794-3139
www.caesars.com/linq/hotel/dining/guy-fieri
CUISINE: Traditional American
DRINKS: Full bar
SERVING: Breakfast, Lunch & Dinner
PRICE RANGE: $$
NEIGHBORHOOD: The Strip
Very busy restaurant and relies heavily on the reputation of celebrity chef Guy Fieri. The place features a predictably gimmicky menu with items like: Brutha's Badass Caesar Salad and the Tatted Up Turkey Burger. The burgers are top notch. Great place for brunch – try the Breakfast Burrito – large

enough to share. Casual atmosphere with lots of TVs. (But for my money, life is too short—and the choices in Vegas too different, creative and numerous—to waste my time in this tourist trap.)

HASH HOUSE A GO GO
3535 Las Vegas Blvd S., Las Vegas: 702-254-4646
http://www.hashhouseagogo.com
CUISINE: American
DRINKS: Full Bar
SERVING: Breakfast/Lunch/Dinner
Hash House A Go Go, located in The LINQ Hotel & Casino, is ideal for those craving a fresh breakfast. Hash House A Go Go specializes in "twisted farm food"; this includes a menu full of fresh dishes with a Mid-Western influence. Start your meal with a selection of juices or premium coffee. Hash House A Go Go also offers unique bloody marys and mimosas like the Blood Orange Crush. With breakfast and brunch being served until 2:00 am on the weekends, there's plenty of time to enjoy a wide selection of favorites at Hash House A Go Go. $$

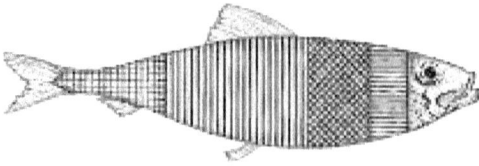

Herringbone

HERRINGBONE
ARIA Resort & Casino
3730 Las Vegas Blvd S, Las Vegas, 702-590-9899
www.herringboneeats.com/las-vegas
CUISINE: American (New), Seafood
DRINKS: Beer & Wine Only
SERVING: Lunch/Dinner
PRICE RANGE: $$$
NEIGHBORHOOD: The Strip
Stylish eatery with a garden patio offering a menu of
sustainable seafood and New American cuisine.
Favorites: Crispy Maryland soft-shell crab served
with sweet corn, Salmon and Seared Tuna. Nice
choice for a romantic dinner or weekend brunch.
More casual than many restaurants on The Strip. Bar
serves crafted cocktails and variety of beers. Sports
TV for game watching.

IL MULINO NEW YORK
3500 Las Vegas Blvd. Suite T30, Las Vegas: 702-
492-6000
www.ilmulino.com
CUISINE: Italian

DRINKS: Full Bar
SERVING: Lunch/Dinner
Located atop Caesar's Palace Forum Shops, Il Mulino offers excellent northern Italian dishes paired with excellent wine and exceptional service. This outpost of the ever-popular Third Avenue-based ristorante is favored by both visitors and locals. Their delicate portions of hors d'oeuvres are rightfully famous as are their daily specials and aromatic menu options. Il Mulino also serves traditional Italian desserts that are among the very best in Las Vegas. $$$$

JEAN GEORGES STEAKHOUSE
ARIA Resort & Casino
3730 Las Vegas Blvd S, Las Vegas, 877-230-2742
www.arialasvegas.com
CUISINE: Steakhouse
DRINKS: Full Bar
SERVING: Dinner
PRICE RANGE: $$$$
NEIGHBORHOOD: The Strip
Sleek upscale steakhouse and lounge but not your typical steakhouse with award-winning chef Jean-Georges Vongerichten at the helm. Newly redecorated, this place still offers a supreme dining experience. A perfect dinner could include the signature Wagyu Carpaccio, a bright tomato salad and a plate of Japanese Snapper with Pickled Cherry Peppers, Mint and Toasted Sesame Seeds…and then there's the steak. You might get similarly high level quality of meat somewhere else, but it won't be better than this. Impressive wine list – note the wall of wine bottles.

JULIAN SERRANO

Aria

3730 Las Vegas Blvd S., Las Vegas: 702-590-8520

www.aria.com/dining/restaurants/julian-serrano

CUISINE: Spanish

DRINKS: Full Bar

SERVING: Lunch/Dinner

Julian Serrano takes his Las Vegas culinary experience to the next level at his new self-titled restaurant, located in the Aria Hotel and Casino. The premiere restaurant for superb tapas on The Strip, Julian Serrano also serves up gourmet paella, seafood, sangria, and atmosphere. The presentation of the Spanish dishes is as elegant as the taste; and with such a diverse menu, diners are bound to find a favorite dish. Being from Miami, and having traveled extensively throughout Spanish language countries, I'm quite familiar with the varied cuisines of Central and South America. But they all hark back to the Spanish classics for their inspiration. So if you're not familiar with Spanish fare, by all means try to work this place into your schedule. You'll be glad you did. Serrano's a genius. $$$

KOI
3667 Las Vegas Blvd. S., Las Vegas: 702-454-4555
http://www.koirestaurant.com
CUISINE: Japanese, Sushi Bars
DRINKS: Full Bar
SERVING: Dinner
Koi at Planet Hollywood combines Las Vegas glitz with Asian exoticism for a distinctly chic dining affair. A Japanese aesthetic blends with a Blade Runner-like futurism to create a stunningly stylish backdrop for the kitchen's Asian food. Intimate niches in booths reminiscent of river rocks reflect the refined naturalism of the bamboo-accented main dining room, while panoramic Strip views ground the restaurant firmly in its cosmopolitan surroundings. The sushi bar serves as a focal point, justifiably drawing attention to Koi's succulent sushi offerings. A bevy of clever Asian and pop culture-inspired beverages enhances the imminently savvy Koi experience. $$$

KUMI JAPANESE RESTAURANT + BAR
Mandalay Place
3950 Las Vegas Blvd S, Las Vegas, 702-632-9100
www.kumilasvegas.com
CUISINE: Japanese/Sushi Bar
DRINKS: Full bar
SERVING: Dinner
PRICE RANGE: $$$
NEIGHBORHOOD: The Strip
This modern twist on an authentic Japanese eatery
offers Chef Akira Back's menu of Japanese fare with
a Korean American twist. Menu picks: Crispy Pork
Belly Roll and Crispy rice with blackened tuna. Great
dining experience.

L'ATELIER DE JOEL ROBUCHON
MGM Grand
3799 S Las Vegas Blvd, Las Vegas, 702-891-7358
www.mgmgrand.com
www.joel-robuchon.net
CUISINE: French
DRINKS: Full bar
SERVING: Dinner
PRICE RANGE: $$$$
NEIGHBORHOOD: The Strip
Tiny eatery (six tables and a counter) but eating at the
counter offers a view of the open kitchen. Menu
courtesy of Chef L'Atelier de Joël Robuchon. Menu
offers gourmet French tapas, a la carte tasting
portions, and a variety of entrees such as Beef with
eggplant and King crab. They are well known among
foodies with the way they treat foie gras – try the

quail stuffed with foie gras served with some of the best mashed potatoes you'll ever scarf down.

LAGO
Bellagio
3600 S Las Vegas Blvd, Las Vegas, 702-693-7111
www.bellagio.com
CUISINE: Italian
DRINKS: Full bar
SERVING: Lunch & Dinner
PRICE RANGE: $$$
NEIGHBORHOOD: The Strip
Elegant eatery offering a creative menu of Italian fare including: pastas, pizzas, focaccia, crostinis, and seafood. Vegetarian options available. Plates are small and meant to be shared. (Good luck with that!) Great views of the fountain show. Reservations recommended.

LE CIRQUE
Bellagio Hotel and Casino
3600 S Las Vegas Blvd, Las Vegas, 702-693-8100
www.bellagio.com
CUISINE: French
DRINKS: Full bar
SERVING: Dinner; closed Mon
PRICE RANGE: $$$$
NEIGHBORHOOD: The Strip
Vegas version of the legendary NYC landmark serving the same innovative New French cuisine. Opulent dining well deserving of its AAA Five Diamond Award rating. Everything is incredible from

the breads to the entrees. Menu favorites: Lobster and Parmesan risotto appetizer and Salmon with asparagus and potato mousselline. Desserts are divine. Impressive wine list. Reservations recommended.

MARGARITAVILLE
3555 Las Vegas Blvd S., Las Vegas: 702-733-3302
http://www.margaritavillelasvegas.com
CUISINE: American
DRINKS: Full Bar
SERVING: Lunch/Dinner
Tourists love this place, but I'm not so big on it. Jimmy Buffett's Margaritaville evokes the island flavor and laid-back fun of its namesake. This whimsical multi-level restaurant offers a variety of lively dining environments for sampling signature margaritas and feasting on tropically-inspired fare like Caribbean Jerk Chicken and Coconut Shrimp. Decorated with palm tree murals, a life size sea plane, and "docked boat" seating, the expansive main dining room tries to impart the feeling of exotic vacation spots, while an upstairs patio offers a cabana-style bar and dining areas with views of The Strip (this is more fun). Popular with groups. $$

MESA GRILL
3570 Las Vegas Blvd. S., Las Vegas: 702-731-7731
www.caesars.com/caesars-palace/restaurants/mesa-grill
CUISINE: Tex-Mex
DRINKS: Full Bar
SERVING: Lunch/Dinner

The first restaurant of celebrity chef Bobby Flay outside of New York is a unique addition to the array of award-winning establishments at Caesars Palace. The 8,800 square foot Southwestern Mesa Grill houses a 28-seat bar and lounge, a three-tiered dining room and an exhibition kitchen. Featuring a pure Southwest cuisine, favorites include the New Mexican spice rubbed pork tenderloin, the filet mignon with the famous coffee-rub and the sweet potato tamale. About his coffee-rubbed steak, Flay says, "Marinades don't leave enough impact. A dry rub packs more flavor and also gives the steak a great crust when seared." So there. $$$

MIZUMI
Wynn Las Vegas
3131 S Las Vegas Blvd, Las Vegas, 702-770-3320
www.wynnlasvegas.com/Dining/FineDining/Mizumi
CUISINE: Japanese
DRINKS: Full bar
SERVING: Dinner
PRICE RANGE: $$$$
NEIGHBORHOOD: The Strip
Chef Devin Hashimoto offers a fresh approach to Japanese cuisine – mixing traditional and contemporary flavors. Menu picks: Tzatziki roll and Kobe steak. One of only a handful of restaurants in the United States serving "certified authentic Kobe beef." Beautiful Japanese garden with a 90-foot waterfall. Reservations recommended.

MR CHOW
Caesars Palace

3570 Las Vegas Blvd, South, Las Vegas, 702-731-7888

www.caesars.com

CUISINE: Chinese

DRINKS: Full bar

SERVING: Dinner

PRICE RANGE: $$$$

NEIGHBORHOOD: The Strip

Recreating the same upscale dining experience as the Mr. Chow in Beverly Hills, this place is ideal for a special occasion or a date. The food is also top notch with menu favorites like: Beijing Duck and Chicken Satay served with hand-pulled Mr. Chow noodles. Take note of the infamous Mr. Chow champagne trolley that is a show unto itself. Reservations recommended.

NINE FINE IRISHMEN

3790 Las Vegas Blvd. S., Las Vegas: 702-740-6463

http://newyorknewyork.com/restaurants/nine-fine-irishmen.aspx

CUISINE: Pubs, Irish

DRINKS: Full Bar

SERVING: Lunch/Dinner

Imagine being able to set foot in an Irish pub without having to leave the country. Here, you can do just that. The bar was built in Ireland, disassembled, and reassembled in the heart of Vegas. Whether you're stopping in for a pint of stout, lingering over a glass of Irish Whiskey, or in for a full meal of traditional Irish fare, Nine Fine Irishmen offers an authentic pub atmosphere. With menu items such as Bangers &

Mash, Shepherd's Pie, and Irish Stew, you'll feel like you're in Dublin. $$

PICASSO
Bellagio Hotel and Casino
3600 S Las Vegas Blvd, Las Vegas, 702-693-8865
www.bellagio.com
CUISINE: French
DRINKS: Full bar
SERVING: Dinner; closed Tues
PRICE RANGE: $$$$
NEIGHBORHOOD: The Strip
Casual eatery but note it's a Michelin two-star restaurant with an excellent wine list so you might want to dress up a bit. Menu picks: Lamb and diver scallops and Wagu and Deer. Inside the restaurant there are real Picasso paintings on the wall (that's what they say) and a view of the big water show outside. Prix-fix menu available.

RED 8 ASIAN BISTRO
3131 Las Vegas Blvd. S., Las Vegas: 702-770-3380
www.wynnlasvegas.com

CUISINE: Chinese
DRINKS: Full Bar
SERVING: Lunch
At Red 8, Chef **Hisham Johari** offers Southeast
Asian cuisine in a casual setting. The extensive menu
offers the best tastes from the region, with such dishes
as a Deep Fried Whole Fish with Soy Ginger Sauce,
Braised Abalone with Seasonal Greens, and
Cantonese Roast Duck. The menu also includes an
extensive selection of rice, noodle, and congee dishes,
and traditional favorites such as Pad Thai Noodles,
Kung Pao Chicken, and Sweet and Sour Pork. $$$

RED SQUARE
Mandalay Bay Hotel
3950 Las Vegas Fwy, Las Vegas, 702-632-7407
www.redsquarelasvegas.com
CUISINE: American (Traditional)
DRINKS: Full bar
SERVING: Dinner
PRICE RANGE: $$$
NEIGHBORHOOD: The Strip
Soviet-themed restaurant and bar complete with ice-
covered bar and private vodka room. Premium
upscale dining experience with great vodka infused
cocktails. Menu picks: Chicken Kiev and Stuffed
Lobster. Two happy hours daily – one early and one
late night.

ROSE RABBIT LIE
COSMOPOLITAN
3708 Las Vegas Blvd S, Las Vegas, 702-698-7440
www.cosmopolitanlasvegas.com

CUISINE: American (New)/Performance bar
DRINKS: Beer & Wine Only
SERVING: Dinner; closed Sun -Tues
PRICE RANGE: $$$$
NEIGHBORHOOD: The Strip
Posh supper club with 10 rooms offers a somewhat scattershot kaleidoscopic entertainment concept styled "Vegas Nocturne." This means some 40 performers mill around doing all sorts of things. There's nothing cheesy about the menu, however. It's superb. Rotating menu often with a theme. Favorites: Short ribs and Beer Can Chicken. Speakeasy-style cocktails. Entertainment throughout your meal such as acrobats performing overhead while you eat. (Classy idea, huh?) Tap dancers on the tables. How about a contortionist shooting off a crossbow with her feet? Here they have it. There's a champagne tower in which the bubbly flows down a stack of 350 coupes. (I hope they use prosecco and not the real stuff.) After your meal, you can stay on for the vaudeville burlesque show in the ballroom. Topless shows are performed at 8, 10 and midnight. Put the little tykes to bed and come back for that one. Reservations needed.

SAGE
ARIA RESORT & CASINO
3732 Las Vegas Blvd S, Las Vegas, 702-590-8690
www.arialasvegas.com
CUISINE: American (New)/Mediterranean
DRINKS: Full Bar
SERVING: Dinner; closed Sundays
PRICE RANGE: $$$$
NEIGHBORHOOD: The Strip

Aria has a handful of highly regarded eateries. One of them is from critically-acclaimed Chef Shawn McClain, who offers a farm-to-table menu of American cuisine with global influences. Menu picks: USDA prime rib cap and Seared & cooked day boat scallops. Cutting-edge mixologists offer a dazzling array of cocktails.

SCARPETTA
The Cosmopolitan of Las Vegas
3708 S Las Vegas Blvd, Las Vegas, 702-698-7960
www.scarpettarestaurants.com/las-vegas
CUISINE: Italian
DRINKS: Full bar
SERVING: Dinner
PRICE RANGE: $$$
NEIGHBORHOOD: The Strip
Modern, intimate restaurant offering an upscale dining experience, especially when you consider that you can enjoy the spectacular Bellagio fountain's water show from a perfect vantage point. Menu picks: Pici and Short Rib Agnolotti. Great breads. Creative crafted cocktails.

SPAGO
3600 Las Vegas Blvd S., Las Vegas: 702-693-8181
www.wolfgangpuck.com/restaurants/fine-dining/9044
CUISINE: American
DRINKS: Full Bar
SERVING: Lunch/Dinner
Spago's Executive Chef Eric Klein wants you to feel as if you're dining in a friend's living room. So Spago's atmosphere is casual. The service is both

impeccable and friendly. The food is simple and unpretentious, yet beautiful. The California-cuisine menu changes daily based on the freshest organic produce. Whether you dine in the cafe known for its pizzas and people watching, or the main dining room known for its steak tartare, Wolfgang Puck's Spago is a winner. $$$

STERLING BRUNCH
3645 Las Vegas Blvd. S., Las Vegas: 702-967-7258
http://www.ballyslasvegas.com/casinos/ballys-las-vegas/restaurants-dining/sterling-brunch-detail.html
CUISINE: Breakfast, Brunch
DRINKS: Full Bar
SERVING: Brunch
At $90 per person, Bally's Sterling Brunch is one of the more expensive buffets in Las Vegas. But the people who have been coming here for 20 years know that Sterling Brunch is not just a great value, it is quite possibly the best value of any restaurant, anywhere. Mountains of oysters. Supersized gulf shrimp cocktails. Endless Maine lobster. Perrier-Jouët champagne flows like a fountain. Caviar, truffles, beef tenderloin, rack of lamb. This is paradise for a gourmand. Sit down and eat a meal that would impress Diamond Jim Brady -- every Sunday, at Bally's. $$$$

TAO ASIAN BISTRO
The Venetian
3377 South Las Vegas Blvd, Las Vegas, 702-388-8338
www.taolasvegas.com

CUISINE: Asian Fusion
DRINKS: Full bar
SERVING: Dinner
PRICE RANGE: $$$
NEIGHBORHOOD: The Strip
Bistro serving Pan-Asian cuisine with a lounge and poolside location for light bites. Menu options: three course meal or family style dining. Menu picks: Peking Duck and Kobe Beef Shabu Shabu. Full sushi bar. Décor is Pacific Rim elegant with velvets and silks, waterfalls and Buddha statues everywhere. Nice assortment of Asian inspired desserts like yoga sugar dusted donuts.

TENDER STEAK & SEAFOOD
3900 Las Vegas Blvd S., Las Vegas: 702-262-4778
http://www.luxor.com/restaurants/tender.aspx
CUISINE: Steakhouse
DRINKS: Full Bar
SERVING: Dinner
This place has been here since 1994 or '95, and ever since then has been winning Las Vegas carnivores over with their fresh, sustainable food and comfortable, masculine decor. Located at the Luxor Las Vegas, it's understated, subdued, and lets the food and the service stand on their own. Their cheese menu has 8 choices, and they always have 3 varieties of oysters. Feel like Surf and Turf Sliders with Kobe beef? No problem. From beef and boar to bison, and seafood to stroganoff, Tender has something for the meat eater in us all. $$$$

TOP OF THE WORLD

2000 Las Vegas Blvd S., Las Vegas: 702-380-7711
http://www.topoftheworldlv.com
CUISINE: American
DRINKS: Full Bar
SERVING: Dinner
Make your next event unforgettable in Top of the
World's private dining rooms. Impress your guests
with breathtaking views and upscale gourmet cuisine.
Private service staff, a personal bartender, customized
menus with on-the-spot entrée selection, VIP entrance
to the tower and complimentary access to the
observation decks are just some of the advantages
when you book a private dining event with
Stratosphere's catering and private dining office. If
you want to show off without going to a nightclub
and buying all the tables bottles of Cristal, this is the
place. $$$$

YELLOWTAIL AT BELLAGIO

Bellagio Hotel and Casino
3600 Las Vegas Blvd Overpass, Las Vegas, 702-730-3900
www.yellowtaillasvegas.com
CUISINE: Japanese/Steakhouse
DRINKS: Full bar
SERVING: Dinner
PRICE RANGE: $$$
NEIGHBORHOOD: The Strip
Known for serving the best traditional and contemporary Japanese cuisine in town. Chef Akira Beak uses only the highest quality ingredients. Menu picks: Big Eye Tuna Pizza and Popping Spicy Crab Roll. Tables overlook the Bellagio Fountains. If you're a celebrity, they'll give you chopsticks with your name printed on them.

WAZUZU

3131 Las Vegas Blvd S., Las Vegas: 702-770-5388
http://www.wynnlasvegas.com/dining/wazuzu
CUISINE: Asian
DRINKS: Full Bar
SERVING: Dinner
Wazuzu in the lavish Encore Hotel and Casino blends the upbeat and energetic atmosphere of Las Vegas with quality Pan-Asian cuisine. Offering dishes from China, Japan, India, Singapore, and Thailand (whew, that covers a lot of geography), Chef Jet Tila provides a unique fusion of dishes and styles, enjoyed under the watchful eye of the crystal dragon that adorns the wall. The décor is fun and exciting, superb for a night

out with friends. The menu has a wide selection of premium sushi and sashimi, as well as an assortment of specialty rolls and a wide variety of Asian favorites. $$$

OFF STRIP

BJ'S RESTAURANT AND BREWHOUSE
10840 W. Charleston Blvd., Las Vegas: 702-853-2300
http://www.bjsrestaurants.com
CUISINE: American
DRINKS: Full Bar
SERVING: Lunch/Dinner
Since 1978, BJ's has shown a respect for the craft of beer, and has created a collection of hand-crafted brews true to their own Chicago-influenced style. Their award-winning house specialty brew called "BJ's Brewhouse Blonde," a light wheat beer with harmonizing tastes of both hops and malt, has earned praises from the California Brewers Association. BJ's boasts at least seven specialty beers per night plus a variety of seasonal beers and special brews. But don't stop there—they also have options for lunch and dinner, featuring an extensive selection of appetizers, soups, salads, Angus burgers, pizza, pasta, and sandwiches. Located across the street from the Red Rock Casino in Summerlin, BJ's Restaurant and Brewery is the prime spot for a casual dining experience. $$

CHINA MAMA

3420 S Jones Blvd, Las Vegas, 702-873-1977
www.chinamamavegas.com
CUISINE: Chinese
DRINKS: No Booze
SERVING: Lunch & Dinner
PRICE RANGE: $$
NEIGHBORHOOD: Chinatown / off Strip
This favorite spot certainly lives up to its reputation
as one of the best Asian eateries in Vegas. Menu
features authentic Chinese fare, Shanghai soup
dumplings (a house specialty), crispy beef, lamb with
cumin and really unforgettable pot stickers.
Great beef wraps and pan fried pork buns.

EATT GOURMET BISTRO

7865 W Sahara Ave, Las Vegas, 702-608-5233
www.eattfood.com
CUISINE: French/Vegan
DRINKS: Wine
SERVING: Lunch/Dinner, Closed Sundays
PRICE RANGE: $$
NEIGHBORHOOD: Via Olivero Springs
Modern French bistro with a bright, fresh, airy feel to
the place. Enormously comfortable & casual. Though
the chefs are French, it doesn't feel very French to
me. But the quality of the preparation is very evident.
Many healthy options. They usually offer 3 or 4 fresh
chilled soups like Gazpacho, Carrot, Borscht.
Favorites: Fish puff pastry for two; Dover Sole; Goat
Cheese Tartine; Duck Breast cooked in grape leaves
making it quite moist and delicious. Menu is seasonal.
Vegan options.

HONEY SALT
1031 S Rampart Blvd, 702-445-6100
www.honeysalt.com
CUISINE: American (New)
DRINKS: Full Bar
SERVING: Lunch/Dinner
PRICE RANGE: $$
NEIGHBORHOOD: Fairway Pointe
Shabby chic New American bistro in a bright airy
room featuring a bar that seats 6 or 8—the rest of the
place is jammed with tables. One long wall is
decorated solely with mirrors of every shape and size.
(I found 3 that I wanted to steal!) Such unusual
shapes. Favorites: Grandma Rosie's Turkey Meatballs
(alta cucina tomatoes, caramelized onions, ricotta);
Sweet Corn Soup; Pan-sealed Scottish salmon and
Fried chicken. Kids' menu. Great selection of
homemade desserts. Reservations recommended.

JAPANESE CURRY ZEN
Suite 1, 5020 Spring Mountain Rd, Las Vegas, 702-
985-1192
www.curryzen.com
CUISINE: Japanese
DRINKS: Full bar
SERVING: Lunch & Dinner
PRICE RANGE: $
NEIGHBORHOOD: Chinatown / off Strip
Japanese eatery offering a fairly simple menu but the
portions are huge so order wisely. Menu picks: Kushi
and any of the Curry dishes. They make their own

garam masala gravy here that they put on almost everything. Popular late-night hangout.

LA STREGA
3555 S Town Center Dr, 702-722-2099
www.lastregalv.com
CUISINE: Italian
DRINKS: Full Bar
SERVING: Dinner, Closed Mondays
PRICE RANGE: $$$
NEIGHBORHOOD: Gardens Park
Somewhat stark and utilitarian interior is still friendly and breezy. Open kitchen. A small bar seats half a dozen patrons. Italian eatery with a menu of signature pasta dishes and pizzas. Menu picks: Anchovy Crostini; Hamachi (chili gremolata, cilantro); Pesto & Truffle Pizza; and Rigatoni Bolognese. Impressive wine list. Sunday brunch.

LAMAII
4480 Spring Mountain Rd, 702-238-0567
www.lamaiilv.com
CUISINE: Thai
DRINKS: Full Bar
SERVING: Lunch/Dinner
PRICE RANGE: $$
NEIGHBORHOOD: Chinatown
Nice interior with bench seating with high tufted backs and heavy chairs. Dark-stained 2x4's mounted vertically divide the seating areas. Wooden shutters, mounted on an otherwise blank wall add a nice touch as they frame nonexistent windows. Curious lighting fixtures hanging above add to the effect. Modern take

on Thai cuisine. Small menu but nice selection. Favorites: Moo Tod Nam Pla (marinated deep-fried pork belly); Kua Gling (ground pork stir fried with curry); Salmon noir and Pad Thai (Chicken/Crispy Prawns). Beautiful place, perfect for date night.

MR. LUCKY'S 24/7
4455 Paradise Rd., Las Vegas: 702-693-5592
http://www.hardrockhotel.com/#/dine/mr-luckys-24-7/
CUISINE: American
DRINKS: Full Bar
SERVING: Breakfast/Lunch/Dinner
While Mr. Lucky's 24/7 may have an unusual name, it serves as a reminder what customers can expect to find anytime day or night. Known for their classic American fare. The "lucky" portion of the restaurant's name comes partially from the fact that Mr. Lucky's is one of the only restaurants to have real gaming machines in the restaurant. Whether customers desire a simple salad or a juicy steak, Mr. Lucky's is eager to offer it in the tastiest way possible. $$

MYUNGRANG HOT DOG
4284 Spring Mountain Rd, 725-214-7286
https://myungranghotdogus.com
CUISINE: Korean Hot Dogs
DRINKS: No Booze
SERVING: Lunch/Dinner
PRICE RANGE: $
NEIGHBORHOOD: Chinatown/Westside

Not your typical hot dog place. Just simple counter service. Only seating is a few stools against the small railing against the wall. These dogs are served on a stick with the dogs deep fried. Incredible variety. Favorites: Mozzarella & Sausage Hot Dog and Rice Cake Hot Dog. Very busy but worth the wait.

NAKAMURA-YA
5040 W Spring Mountain Rd Suite 5, Las Vegas, 702-251-0022
www.nakamurayalv.com/
CUISINE: Italian/Japanese
DRINKS: Full bar
SERVING: Lunch & Dinner
PRICE RANGE: $$$
NEIGHBORHOOD: Chinatown / off Strip
Small cozy eatery offering a unique Japanese/Italian mixture, or really it's Japanese style pasta (that you don't usually see outside Japan), with some Italian influences. Unique dishes like: Miso carbonara spaghetti and Salmon Carpaccio. For dessert try Nakamura-Ya's 3 Dessert Sampler. Expect a wait for a table.

NOBU
4455 Paradise Rd., Las Vegas: 702-693-5090
https://noburestaurants.com
CUISINE: Japanese, Sushi Bars
DRINKS: Full Bar
SERVING: Dinner
Nobu, inside the Hard Rock Hotel and Casino, brings the allure of finely crafted Japanese fare to the Nevada desert. Executive Chef Nobu Matsuhisa

balances classic Japanese technique with innovative flavor and ingredient combinations to create a satisfying fusion of East and West. This tasty marriage of elements can be seen in dishes like the popular Fresh Yellowtail Sashimi with Jalapeno. Nobu's inspiring cuisine is enjoyed within a similarly rousing space designed by David Rockwell himself. The hand-laid river rock wall feature is a highlight for guests, and other design elements like room dividers made of bamboo fronds create a lusciously serene atmosphere in which to dine. $$$$

PHO 87
Phoenix Plaza VII
3620 S Jones Blvd, Las Vegas, 702-233-8787
www.pho87.net
CUISINE: Vietnamese
DRINKS: Full bar
SERVING: Lunch & Dinner; closed Wed
PRICE RANGE: $$
NEIGHBORHOOD: Chinatown / off Strip
A family-run eatery specializing in pho (broth/soup). Unusual atmosphere, but it's basically a Vietnamese buffet that sells health oriented products. This place is known for its food, not for its service.

PING PANG PONG
Gold Coast Hotel and Casino Las Vegas
4000 W Flamingo Rd, Las Vegas, 702-367-7111
www.goldcoastcasino.com
CUISINE: Dim Sum/Seafood/Cantonese
DRINKS: Full bar
SERVING: Lunch & Dinner, Brunch

PRICE RANGE: $$$
NEIGHBORHOOD: 1 mile from the Strip and Chinatown.
A favorite of locals who love Dim Sum, and this is no doubt the best in the city. There's usually a line during rush hour. Busy always with people nursing hangovers. Menu features a variety of dim sum, seafood, and traditional Chinese regional dishes. Favorites include: Har Gow (shrimp balls), Siu Mai (steaming dumplings) and Spare ribs. Nice choice for Sunday Brunch.

RAKU
5030 Spring Mountain Rd, 702-367-3511
http://raku-grill.com/grill/
CUISINE: Japanese
DRINKS: Beer, Wine, & Sake
SERVING: Dinner, Closed Sundays
PRICE RANGE: $$$
NEIGHBORHOOD: Westside
Small eatery with an atmosphere so dark and solemn it feels quite ascetic, even claustrophobic. But where everything looks dark and gloomy, there's more than enough to celebrate in the food here. The place offers a VERY creative menu of Japanese fare (not nigiri or sushi), as evidenced by the blackboard where they list the freshest fish they can get. I always bring someone with me who knows more about Japanese food (really good Japanese food, that is) than I do. I am always rewarded for doing this by getting the best things they have to offer. Favorites: Grilled king crab; Kurobuta Pork Cheek; Oyaji tofu. They have an Omakase menu that comes with Fried chicken, and boy, is it good!.

Nice wine and sake selection. Reservations recommended.

DOWNTOWN

CARSON KITCHEN
124 S 6th St #100, Las Vegas, 702-473-9523
www.carsonkitchen.com
CUISINE: Modern American
DRINKS: Full bar
SERVING: Lunch & Dinner; closed Sun
PRICE RANGE: $$
NEIGHBORHOOD: Downtown
Comfortable eatery serving up modern American comfort food including gourmet burgers, flatbreads, lamb chops and gyro tacos. The deviled eggs here are topped off with bacon and caviar—the best deviled eggs ever. For dessert, if there's room, try the doughnut bread pudding. (It sounds like it would make sure sick—until you taste it.)

CHICAGO BREWING COMPANY
2201 S. Fort Apache Rd., Las Vegas: 702-254-3333
www.chicagobrewinglv.com/
CUISINE: American
DRINKS: Full Bar
SERVING: Lunch/Dinner
Located in the Four Queens Casino. A great selection of handcrafted micro brews to quench the thirst of any diner. What thirst, you ask? The thirst provided

by the selection of delectably deep-fried appetizers, that's what thirst. Or for those with more of an appetite, they have pizzas, including their signature Chicago Deep Dish with sausage and pepperoni. In addition to these heavy offerings, there are also salads, sandwiches, and wraps available. After your meal, choose from Chicago Brewing Company's selection of fine cigars and enjoy another beer in this man's oasis. $$

FLOCK & FOWL
150 N Las Vegas Blvd, 702-272-2222
www.flockandfowl.com
CUISINE: American (New) / Asian Fusion / Singaporean
DRINKS: Full Bar
SERVING: Lunch/Dinner
PRICE RANGE: $$
NEIGHBORHOOD: Downtown
Very colorful Asian wallpaper against one wall lightens up this small eatery offering a menu of Chinese cuisine with subtle twists from Singapore. Sit at the bar, or at tables against the glass walls, or outside, but you'll be sitting there overlooking a boring parking lot, so it's better inside. Lots of vegan choices. Menu picks: Buttermilk Fried Chicken Bao; Hainan chicken; and BBQ Pork bao. Award-winning crafted cocktails and locally brewed beers.

HATSUMI
Ferguson's Motel
1028 Fremont St, 702-268-8939

www.hatsumilv.com
CUISINE: Japanese
DRINKS: Beer & Wine
SERVING: Dinner, Closed Tues & Wed.
PRICE RANGE: $$
NEIGHBORHOOD: Downtown/Freemont Street
Part of Fergusons/Downtown, a funky little place that features rooms decorated by local artists, you'll find this small eatery with a bar on one side of the narrow room and a few rough wooden booths against the wall. Offers a unique take on Japanese street food. Robata Izakaya style dining with a Yakatori Bar. Favorites: Crispy Quail; Pig Ear; Chicken Meatballs; Poached Chicken salad. Impressive sake & wine list.

LA COMIDA
100 S 6th St, Las Vegas, 702-463-9900
www.lacomidalv.com
CUISINE: Mexican
DRINKS: Full bar
SERVING: Lunch & Dinner
PRICE RANGE: $$
NEIGHBORHOOD: Downtown
Modern eatery offers a menu of creative Mexican fare, which is really street food taken to another, much higher, level. Great selection of margaritas and tequilas.

PIZZA ROCK
201 N 3rd St, 702-385-0838
www.pizzarocklasvegas.com
CUISINE: Pizza / Italian
DRINKS: Full Bar

SERVING: Lunch/Dinner
PRICE RANGE: $$
NEIGHBORHOOD: Fremont Street
Hip eatery (there's a huge semi truck that's part of the interior4 décor) offering an amazing selection of gourmet pies all cooked in their 700-degree electric brick oven. They have other Italian specialties if you don't want pizza, but the pizza is the best. Charcuterie boards; Beer Battered Artichokes; Honey Calabrese Sausage; Pizza in both the Napoletana and Romana styles. Vegan/Gluten-free options. Crafted cocktails and beers. Games, DJ nights.

OTHER

MARCHÉ BACCHUS
2620 Regatta Dr Ste 106, Las Vegas, 702-804-8008
www.marchebacchus.com
CUISINE: French
DRINKS: Full bar
SERVING: Lunch & Dinner
PRICE RANGE: $$$
NEIGHBORHOOD: Summerlin
Upscale French bistro with an outdoor patio. Menu features classic and contemporary French fare. Menu picks: Swordfish and Pork Loin. Impressive wine list with over 950 labels to choose from. Nice dessert selection. Good choice for Sunday brunch.

BUFFETS

Yes, the groaning buffet smorgasbord is a time-honored tradition in Vegas. But the days of the $2.95 breakfast and the $5.95 dinner are long-gone.

Do yourself a favor, however, and walk around the buffet before you plunge in.

Take special care to have a look at the dessert spread before you begin. You will surely find something you'll want to save room for. So remember: save room.

Another tip: don't simply load up on the roast beef and potatoes. Here's a chance for you to try dozens of different foods you might not have had in a while—or ever.

So choose small portions so you can savor a lot of different foods, rather than pig-out on one or two items.

Another good way buffets can help the budget-minded: eat later in the day and make one meal count for two.

BAYSIDE BUFFET
Mandalay Bay, 3950 Las Vegas Blvd. S., Las Vegas: 877-632-7800
http://www.mandalaybay.com/dining/quick-eats/bayside-buffet.aspx
Breakfast, 7-11.
Lunch, 11-2:30
Dinner, 4:45-9:45.
Brunch, 7-4:30
Though the room is big (it can hold 500), the way they've laid it out in little nooks and crannies gives the place a very intimate feeling. Floor-to-ceiling windows offer sweeping views of the lush tropical garden outside that fills over 10 acres.

BUFFET AT THE BELLAGIO
3600 Las Vegas Blvd S., Las Vegas: 702-693-8111
http://www.bellagio.com/restaurants/the-buffet.aspx
Breakfast, 7-11
Lunch, 11-3
Dinner, 3-10,
Weekend Brunch, 7-3
The buffet incorporates several cooking stations and a level of food quality and presentation that will impress you. Cuisines offered include Italian,

Japanese, Chinese, seafood and American. Kobe beef, leg of lamb, Mako shark, fresh tuna and even game like venison. No smoking here. (Check their policy on kids: you have to be a hotel guest to get in under 18.)

BUFFET AT WYNN'S
3131 Las Vegas Blvd S., Las Vegas: 702-770-3340
http://www.wynnlasvegas.com/dining/casual-dining
Breakfast: Monday through Friday, 8-11.
Lunch: Monday through Friday, 11-3.
Dinner: Sunday through Thursday, 3:30 to 10.
Friday and Saturday, 3:30 to 10:30.
Sunday, 3:30 to 10.
Champagne Brunch: Saturday and Sunday, 8-3.
They have 16 cooking stations. Specialties are American, Mexican, Southern, Sushi and Italian. Glazed salmon, steamed mussels, king crab legs, rack of lamb, grilled vegetables, and pesto mashed potatoes. No smoking. Like everything else Wynn does, this is over the top.

CARNIVAL WORLD BUFFET AT RIO

3700 Flamingo Rd West, Las Vegas: 702-777-7757
http://www.riolasvegas.com/casinos/rio/restaurants-dining/carnival-world-buffet-detail.html
Lunch 11-3
Dinner 3-10
Weekend Brunch, 8-3
More than 300 dishes prepared fresh daily and a new contemporary design. From pizza to omelets, sushi to teppan yaki, fresh carved meats to Asian barbecue, the Carnival World Buffet offers numerous distinct dining experiences from around the world featuring cooking stations. Dessert? More than 70 varieties of homemade pies, cakes and pastries, and nine gelato flavors, all made from scratch.

CRAVINGS BUFFET AT MIRAGE

3400 Las Vegas Blvd. S., Las Vegas: 702-791-7111
http://www.mirage.com/restaurants/cravings.aspx
Breakfast, Mon-Fri, 7-11
Midweek Brunch, Mon-Fri, 11-3
Dinner, daily, 3-9
Weekend Brunch, 8-3, (including Champagne).
Striped carpeting gives this place a whimsical look (it also reminds me of some of that awful carpeting you sometimes see on cruise ships), but it's all about the food. They offer 11 cooking stations. Focus is on Asian, Italian, Japanese, sushi, seafood, salads and desserts.

FEAST BUFFET

2300 Paseo Verde Pkwy., Henderson: 702-617-7777

http://www.greenvalleyranchresort.com/dining/feast-buffet.php
Breakfast, 8-10:45
Lunch, 11-3
Dinner, 4-9
Sunday Brunch, 8-3
Has 6 cooking stations serving Italian, American, Mongolian, Chinese and "International specialties." They toot their big selection of low-carb menu items. (Of course, what in God's holy name would you be doing at a buffet if you were on a diet?) Best thing about this buffet is the price. Nothing else makes it stand out.

FLAVORS AT HARRAH'S
3475 Las Vegas Blvd., S., Las Vegas: 702-369-5000
http://www.harrahslasvegas.com/casinos/harrahs-las-vegas/restaurants-dining/flavors-the-buffet-detail.html
Breakfast, 7-11
Lunch weekdays, 11-4
Dinner Daily, 3-10
Dinner Fri, Sat, 4-9:30
Sat & Sun Brunch 10 - 4
Children: discounted.
Cooking stations offer freshly prepared seafood, all-you-can-eat crab legs and fresh cut Prime Rib, dozens of side dishes, traditional comfort foods and a variety of pastries. Has cuisines from around the world, including Churrasco (Brazilian BBQ), great pizzas and Italian casseroles prepared in a wood burning oven, fire-roasted rotisserie chicken, steamed crab legs and tasty Asian selections such as hand rolled-

sushi, Maki Rolls and homemade wonton soup as well as traditional Southwestern dishes. Dessert standout: they offer a gelato station with homemade sorbet, gelato and ice cream.

GARDEN COURT BUFFET
200 N. Main Street, Las Vegas: 702-387-1896
http://www.mainstreetcasino.com/dining/garden-court-buffet
CUISINE: Buffet
DRINKS: Beer/Wine
SERVING: Breakfast/Lunch/Dinner
Breakfast, 7-10:30
Lunch, 11-3
Champagne Brunch (Sat & Sun), 7-3
Dinner (Sun), 4-10
Dinner (Mon-Thurs), 4-9
Friday Seafood Buffet, 4-10
Saturday Prime Rib & Scampi Special, 4-10
The variety and quality of the Victorian-style Garden Court Buffet, located inside Main Street Station, has risen to the challenge of becoming one of the best in the downtown area. With a very spacious interior, diners can expect to find 9 cooking stations where cuisines represented include Chinese, Mexican and Italian. A "specialty theme" runs each day of the week, highlighting a particular main course. $$

GRAND BUFFET AT MGM
3799 Las Vegas Blvd. S., Las Vegas: 702-891-7433
http://www.mgmgrand.com/restaurants/mgm-grand-buffet.aspx
Breakfast, 7-10:30

Lunch, 10:30-3
Dinner, Mon-Sun, 3-9:30
Weekend Champagne Brunch, 7-3
Here they have what they call "signature dishes," and
they're very nice: Prime Rib roast, oven roasted
turkey, fresh giant shrimp, Alaskan King crab legs
and steak and fish grilled to order. (The prime ribs
and king crabs legs are at dinner only.) Burgundy
short ribs (lunch only), Osso Buco (dinner only),
shrimp and wild mushroom ravioli. Before or after
you gorge yourself into a coma, check out the rather
interesting display of glass jars.

LE VILLAGE BUFFET AT PARIS
3655 Las Vegas Blvd. S., Las Vegas: 702-946-7000
http://www.parislasvegas.com/casinos/paris-las-
vegas/restaurants-dining/village-buffet-detail.html
Breakfast, Mon-Fri, 7-11
Breakfast, Sat, Sun, 7-10
Lunch, Mon-Fri, 11-3
Dinner, Weekdays, 3-10

Dinner, Weekends, 3-11

Saturday & Sunday Champagne Brunch 10-3

Somewhat different with its French village settings. What they try for here is to bring to life five French provinces by combining the food from that province with a very impressive detailed visual environment. So, each station is themed for a particular province and features an intricate facade designed to replicate the architecture of that region. Meals are prepared to order. A large selection of pastries, pies and an assortment of sugar-free delicacies are offered from the buffet's dessert station. You'll dine in a village-like setting, where you may choose to eat outside in the "town square" or in a casual dining room by a fireplace. (I love to see fireplaces in Vegas!) Each province's cottage dining room is decorated for the region. (This is my favorite buffet after the MGM Grand.)

PARADISE GARDEN BUFFET AT FLAMINGO

3555 Las Vegas Blvd. S., Las Vegas: 702-733-3111

http://www.flamingolasvegas.com/casinos/flamingo-las-vegas/restaurants-dining/paradise-garden-buffet-detail.html

Breakfast, Mon-Fri., 7-11

Breakfast, Sat-Sun, 7-10

Lunch, Mon-Fri, 11-2

Dinner, nightly, 5-10

Brunch, Sat-Sun, 10-2

Here you can watch the playful antics of some of the Flamingo's legendary wildlife outside the windows overlooking the Garden. Fresh fruit bar, mounds of shrimp on ice, snow crab legs (dinner), sushi (lunch and dinner). Carving stations serve herb crusted prime rib of beef and slow-roasted breast of turkey, leg of spring lamb, miso glazed duck, sautéed clams and mussels, double breaded Southern fried chicken, chef's catch of the day and more. Dessert bar has an ice cream sundae station along with freshly baked pies, cakes, pudding and pastries. The breakfast buffet includes more than 60 items: made-to-order omelets, honey-glazed ham, smoked Norwegian salmon, roasted breakfast sausage, smokehouse bacon, buttermilk biscuits, made-to-order malted waffles, country-fried potatoes and freshly baked pastries.

SPICE MARKET BUFFET AT PLANET HOLLYWOOD
3667 Las Vegas Blvd. S., Las Vegas: 702-785-5555
http://www.planethollywoodresort.com/casinos/planet-hollywood/restaurants-dining/spice-market-buffet-detail.html
Breakfast, Mon-Fri, 7-11
Breakfast, Sat-Sun, 7-10
Lunch daily, 11-3
Dinner daily, 3-11
Weekend Brunch, 10-3
Cuisines: Asian, Mexican, Italian, Middle Eastern, American. And the ubiquitous crab legs that for some reason everybody thinks are so great. (I can't stand them—too messy.)

Chapter 4
NIGHTLIFE

GENERAL LISTINGS

DISCOUNT TICKETS

Company called **Tix4Tonight** that sells discount tickets to almost every show, often at half the box office price. http://www.tix4tonight.com. I wouldn't be surprised to find out they sell more tickets to the shows than the hotels do themselves. I've never used anybody but these people. And even if others are paying, I do them a favor and give them this web site. (They also offer steep discounts on some big hotels.)

1 OAK
Mirage
3400 Las Vegas Blvd. S., Las Vegas: 702-792-7900

www.1oaklasvegas.com

Hot new club at the Mirage is a sister act to the 1 OAK in New York. A swank design with original artwork by Roy Nachum, the 16,000 square foot space has all the usual amenities one expects at a major Vegas club, but sports a more mature attitude. Excellent sound system worked by DJs brought in from all over the world to keep the pretty people bouncing away the night on the dance floor.

CASA FUENTE

The Forum Shops at Caesars
3500 S Las Vegas Blvd S 08, Las Vegas, 702-731-5051
www.casafuente.com
NEIGHBORHOOD: The Strip
Men's cigar lounge that offers cocktails and a whole lot more besides. This place is for cigar aficionados and sells a variety of cigars and accessories (cutters, lighters, etc) for your smoking pleasure, as they used to say before everybody died of cancer. (The Fuente family have been making quality cigars for a hundred years or more.) Lounge features a humidor room and gift shop. Has an Old World men's club vibe for cocktails & coffee over cigars. Settle in for a single malt and a good smoke.

CHATEAU

3655 Las Vegas Blvd., Las Vegas: 702-776-7777
www.chateaunights.com
Tue, Fri-Sun 10 pm - 4:30 am
This massive nightclub on The Strip, that rises two floors, has three different areas where you get the

feeling you've been to three different clubs. (They don't want you going anywhere!) Very high energy. Unparalleled views of The Strip.

COMMONWEALTH
525 Fremont St, Las Vegas, 702-445-6400
www.commonwealthlv.com
NEIGHBORHOOD: Downtown
Hipster cocktail lounge featuring live music, DJs, rooftop bar, medium sized dance floor and a members-only "secret" bar. Great hand-crafted cocktails.

COYOTE UGLY SALOON
3790 Las Vegas Blvd S., Las Vegas: 702-740-6969
www.coyoteuglysaloon.com
Mon-Sun 6 pm - 4 am
Adult entertainment. You know the movie. Here you can see the real thing—live. Watch how the bartenders do their job.

FOUNDATION ROOM
3950 Las Vegas Blvd S., Las Vegas: 702-632-7631
www.houseofblues.com/lasvegas/fr
The dance club / lounge is members-only room that rests on top of the Mandalay Bay, so from here (if you have a friend who can get you in) you can see unrivaled views of The Strip. You'll find really great dining in here, an elegant lounge area, and several private rooms for more intimate entertaining. Tip: if you're not a member and you're in town on Monday, they allow the public in when the place becomes an after-hours club called "Godspeed."

OAK & IVY
Downtown Container Park
707 Fremont St, Las Vegas, 702-553-2549
www.oakandivy.com
NEIGHBORHOOD: Downtown
Fans of crafted cocktails love this place. This is
primarily an American craft whiskey cocktail bar
featuring classic and unique handcrafted cocktails.
Nice selection of rare beers. Great place to relax and
enjoy a cocktail in a quiet atmosphere.

PETROSSIAN
Bellagio Hotel
3600 Las Vegas Fwy, Las Vegas, 702-693-7111
https://www.bellagio.com/en/nightlife/petrossian-
bar.html
NEIGHBORHOOD: The Strip
Want to party all night, then this is your place. Open
24 hours (except Sunday, when it's closed). This
upscale lounge features champagne, caviar, English
tea service, luxury appetizers, and wonderfully
crafted cocktails. Live piano music.

Cirque de Soleil Shows

THE BEATLES LOVE
The Mirage

3400 S. Las Vegas Blvd., Las Vegas: 702-792-7777
http://www.mirage.com
With LOVE, Cirque du Soleil celebrates the musical legacy of The Beatles through their timeless, original recordings. Using the master tapes at Abbey Road Studios, Sir George Martin and his son Giles Martin have created a unique soundscape of Beatles music for the show. The exuberance of the Beatles is channeled through the youthful, urban energy of a cast of 60 international artists. With panoramic sound and visuals, the audience experience is impressive.

CRISS ANGEL MINDFREAK
PLANET HOLLYWOOD
3667 Las Vegas Blvd. S., Las Vegas: 702-777-2782
https://crissangel.com/planet-hollywood-mindfreak/
Criss Angel offers an illusion spectacular based at Planet Hollywood. Recently awarded Magician of the Century, Criss Angel brings his arsenal of magic feats that truly delve deep into the minds of audience members and leave guests in a state of bewilderment, awe and fascination.

KÁ
MGM Grand
3799 S. Las Vegas Blvd, Las Vegas: 866-740-7711
http://www.mgmgrand.com
Experience the unbelievable at KÁ, a heroic tale of
twins who embark on an adventurous journey to
fulfill their destinies. Featuring 80 artists from around
the world, KÁ by Cirque du Soleil is a gravity-
defying production featuring acrobatic feats, Capoeira
dance and martial arts, and can only be seen at MGM
Grand.

MICHAEL JACKSON ONE
Mandalay Bay
3950 S. Las Vegas Blvd., Las Vegas: 702-632-7777
www.mandalaybay.com
An incredible tribute to the legendary Michael
Jackson with an amazing show that combines dance,

music and awe-inspiring visuals. Filled with Michael's powerful music in a state-of-the-art surround-sound environment, this multi-layered production features a vibrant cast of 63 dancers and performers. The non-stop show is filled with vivid choreography, driving acrobatics, and breathtaking aerial performances.

MYSTÈRE

Treasure Island
3300 S. Las Vegas Blvd., Las Vegas: 702-894-7722
http://www.treasureisland.com
Mystère is a classic Cirque du Soleil production that combines powerful athleticism, high-energy acrobatics and inspiring imagery. The vibrant stage of Mystère is punctuated by colorful costumes and signature Cirque du Soleil acts such as Chinese Poles, Hand to Hand balancing, Aerial High Bar and Bungee. Presented exclusively at Treasure Island.

O AT BELLAGIO

3600 Las Vegas Blvd. S., Las Vegas: 702-693-7111
http://www.bellagio.com
Cirque du Soleil paints an aquatic masterpiece of surrealism and theatrical romance in the timeless production, "O." The international cast of world-class acrobats, synchronized swimmers, divers and aerialists perform in, on, and above water, creating a seamless and ever-changing canvas of tableaus.

ZUMANITY
AT NEW YORK-NEW YORK
3790 Las Vegas Blvd. S., Las Vegas: 866-606-7111
http://newyorknewyork.com
ZUMANITY unveils the sensual side of Cirque du
Soleil. This mischievous production blends playful
innuendo with daring eroticism in the intimate
ZUMANITY Theatre. A provocative cabaret-style
production, ZUMANITY features outrageous humor,
alluring acrobatics and intoxicating dance set to the
pulse of intoxicating rhythms.

Comedy Clubs

BRAD GARRETT'S COMEDY CLUB
MGM Grand
3799 Las Vegas Blvd. S., Las Vegas: 866-740-7711
www.mgmgrand.com
This venue features a never-ending line-up of the
finest comedians around – from established stand-up
stars to the hottest young comics in the business. The
only location in Las Vegas where you can see Brad

Garrett perform and he may even greet you at the door. Nightly at 8 pm.

FOUR QUEENS L.A. COMEDY CLUB
202 E Fremont St., Las Vegas: 702-385-4011
http://www.fourqueens.com
For an evening of laughter, you won't want to miss this place. The price of admission won't break you. The entertainment is always hilarious, as headlining comedians are matched with Las Vegas talent. Afternoon and evening shows, comedy, hypnotist, magic, special tributes and headlining comedians.

V THEATRE
Planet Hollywood
3663 Las Vegas Blvd, Las Vegas, 866-932-1818
http://www.planethollywoodresort.com
Sin City. Comedy. Beautiful girls and famous comedians take the stage when this hilarious show combines sexy burlesque with world-class stand up comedy in a choreographed production of music & fun. Hot ladies of the Sin City Dollz perform

seductive dance numbers and two headliner comics keep audiences rolling in the aisles with laughter.

Chapter 5
THE CASINOS

ARIA LAS VEGAS
3730 Las Vegas Blvd., Las Vegas: 702-590-7111
http://www.arialasvegas.com
Thousands of slots (traditional reel, video, and server based) of all denominations, dozens of table games, two high limit lounges, a race and sports book, and a poker room. Also the newest casino in town.

BALLY'S
3645 Las Vegas Blvd S., Las Vegas: 702-967-4111
http://www.ballyslasvegas.com
The newly remodeled, 67,000-square-foot casino delivers a bright and lively gaming area loaded with

all the traditional games. From the latest games to the best casino classics, there's no shortage of action on Bally's vibrant casino floor.

BELLAGIO
3600 Las Vegas Blvd S., Las Vegas: 888-987-6667
http://www.bellagio.com
Unparalleled Five Diamond Award-winning action is dealt with the utmost sophistication at this stylish Las Vegas casino. From dramatic touches to Bellagio's casino, which features a variety of slots, table games, and Race & Sports Book wagering to the World Poker Tour.

CAESARS PALACE
3570 Las Vegas Blvd S., Las Vegas: 866-227-5938
http://www.caesarspalace.com
Caesars Palace is a modern-day Roman Empire that will dazzle you with unparalleled excitement and challenge your every skill with games of chance. Caesars Palace has been the site of more million-dollar plus slot machine jackpots than any casino in the world.

CIRCUS CIRCUS
2880 Las Vegas Blvd S., Las Vegas: 702-734-0410
http://www.circuscircus.com
The newly remodeled Race & Sports Book is a super-charged hangout for sports fans. Watch all the action on their 32 large-screen Hi-Def TV's, ranging from 52" to their giant 103" screen, which always shows the featured game of the day.

GOLD COAST HOTEL & CASINO

4000 W Flamingo Rd., Las Vegas: 702-367-7111
http://www.goldcoastcasino.com
More than 86,000 square feet of fast-paced action
including 48 tables featuring Craps, Blackjack, Pai
Gow Poker, Super Fun 21, Roulette and Mini and
Midi Baccarat. Non-smoking Poker Room. Or bet
your favorites in the spacious race and sports book or
head upstairs to the lavish 720-seat bingo room. Plus
more than 2,100 of the most popular slot and video
poker machines.

LUXOR LAS VEGAS

3900 Las Vegas Blvd. S., Las Vegas: 702-262-4000
http://www.luxor.com
The dealers at the Luxor card room are very good as
is the wait staff. Comps at the poker card room
include free drinks while playing at the tables. Play is
average and this is one of the best rooms for beginner
players to try their luck. The casino also offers their
poker players lessons every afternoon if they are

interested in learning more about the game. The room's location is fairly isolated but it is close to the sports book which occasionally gets a bit rowdy, especially during football season.

MANDALAY BAY
3950 Las Vegas Blvd. S. Las Vegas: 702-632-7777
http://www.mandalaybay.com
Slots are one of the icons Las Vegas is best known for. With over 2,000 slot and video poker machines to choose from, you'll find a full selection of your favorite games. Mandalay Bay offers a variety of games ranging from $0.01 to $100.

MGM GRAND
3799 Las Vegas Blvd S., Las Vegas: 877-880-0880
http://www.mgmgrand.com

With denominations ranging from 1¢ to $1,000, they offer thousands of slots, video poker, and multi-game machines. MGM also has custom machines that you won't find anywhere else in Las Vegas. Majestic Lions is their most popular $1 progressive machine, paying out over $750,000 each day. Want more? For a chance to win $1,000,000, take their exclusive Reel Millions and Lion's Share machines for a spin.

THE MIRAGE
3400 Las Vegas Blvd S., Las Vegas: 702-791-7111
http://www.mirage.com
The Mirage slot player has hundreds of options from which to choose. Interactive slots, multi-line machines, traditional "reel" slot machines and the latest video reel machines on the market. Players may go after single machine progressives, or try for the big bucks on one of their machines with a multi-million dollar top award. The Mirage has non-smoking tables available.

NEW YORK-NEW YORK
3790 Las Vegas Blvd S., Las Vegas: 702-740-6969
http://newyorknewyork.com
Try your hand at more than 1,500 slots in varying denominations including:
Wheel of Fortune, Megabucks, Jackpot Party, Blazing 7's, Top Dollar, Sex & the City, Monopoly and Goldfish. The casino offers 84,000 square feet of space with more than 67 gaming tables.

THE ORLEANS HOTEL & CASINO
4500 W Tropicana Ave., Las Vegas: 702-365-7111

http://www.orleanscasino.com
Over 3,000 slots, video poker and video keno
machines. Blackjack, Craps, Roulette, Pai Gow
Poker, Baccarat, Let It Ride and Three Card Poker,
Race and Sports Book, the 35-table Poker Room, and
the 24-Hour, 60-seat Keno Lounge. Be sure to join
the exclusive B Connected and earn valuable benefits.

PARK MGM
3770 Las Vegas Blvd S., Las Vegas: 702-730-7777
www.parkmgm.com
Park MGM is slot machine heaven. Choose from
traditional slots to the latest video poker machines.
Go after single-machine progressives or take a spin
for the big bucks on one of the multimillion-dollar
jackpot slots. Whatever your pleasure, there's always
the perfect spot to pull up a comfy stool and see if
today is your lucky one. Table games are the heart
and soul of classic casino action, and Park MGM has
all your favorites. Whether you're in the mood for a
simple, elegant game of Baccarat or the rowdy action
at the craps table, you'll find it all here.

PARIS
3655 Las Vegas Blvd S., Las Vegas: 702-946-7000
http://www.parislasvegas.com
Slot machines and video games. Megabucks
progressives, reel slots and multi-line video slots.
Cobblestone pathways and iron streetlamps.

PALMS
4321 W Flamingo Rd., Las Vegas: 702-942-7777
http://www.palms.com

From lower limits to high stakes, you'll find it all at the Palms Poker tables.

The Poker room features $2-$4 and $4-$8 Limit Texas Hold 'Em with a half kill. Higher limit spread upon request.

Noted as the best paying slots in Vegas by the Las Vegas Review Journal's "Best of Las Vegas."

PLANET HOLLYWOOD HOTEL & CASINO

3667 Las Vegas Blvd S., Las Vegas: 866-919-7472
http://www.planethollywoodresort.com
With a wide variety of games and denominations, including penny slots, video reels, video poker and other fun and popular variations.

RED ROCK CASINO RESORT & SPA

11011 W Charleston Blvd., Las Vegas: 702-797-7777
http://www.redrocklasvegas.com
A dedicated room for the ultimate in poker gaming, the Poker Room allows you to bluff to your heart's content in comfortable, modern surroundings. Open 24 hours, the poker room features a variety of tables offering Texas Hold 'Em, Omaha and more.

RIO
3700 W Flamingo Rd., Las Vegas: 866-746-7671
http://www.riolasvegas.com
The Rio's world-class amenities include more than
100,000 square feet of gaming space, hosting around
1,200 state-of-the-art slot and video poker machines,
more than 80 table games including blackjack, craps,
Baccarat, roulette, Let It Ride, Caribbean Stud Poker
and Mini-Baccarat as well as a Keno Lounge, and a
full-service Race & Sports Book.

SAM'S TOWN
5111 Boulder Hwy, Las Vegas: 702-456-7777
http://www.samstownlv.com
Catch all the action on 60 big screen TVs, all
surrounded with comfortable seating, a snack bar,
even free cocktail service. Bet on all your favorite
professional and college sports teams or wager on a

horse or dog race with their no-limit, pari-mutuel wagering.

STRATOSPHERE
2000 Las Vegas Blvd S., Las Vegas: 702-380-7777
http://www.stratospherehotel.com
This Las Vegas casino features over 1,200 slot and video poker games.

TROPICANA
3801 Las Vegas Blvd S., Las Vegas: 702-739-2222
http://www.troplv.com
The newly transformed Las Vegas Casino features over 800 slots. Wheel of Fortune, Gold Fish, Wolf Run and table games at one of The Strip's classic casinos. Classic Blackjack. Cheering Craps tables. Spinning Roulette wheels.

TREASURE ISLAND
3300 Las Vegas Blvd S., Las Vegas: 702-894-7111
http://www.treasureisland.com
Treasure Island offers all the classic table games of a top-notch Las Vegas casino, including a generous selection of challenging table games for seasoned players, as well as beginner-friendly choices for newcomers.

WESTGATE RESORT & CASINO
3000 Paradise Rd., Las Vegas: 702-732-5111
www.thelvh.com
From Baccarat and Blackjack to Craps and Roulette, their table games make them a premier choice among outstanding casinos in Las Vegas.

Chapter 6
ATTRACTIONS

GENERAL LISTINGS

AQUARIUM AT THE MIRAGE
3400 Las Vegas Boulevard S., Las Vegas: 702-791-7111.
http://www.mirage.com/attractions/aquarium.aspx
Behind the front desk at the Mirage you'll see a
20,000-gallon saltwater aquarium. Managed by The
Mirage's own in-house aquarists, the aquarium
accommodates more than 1,000 coral reef animals
representing 60 species from Australia, Hawaii,
Tonga, Fiji, the Red Sea, the Marshall Islands, the
Sea of Cortez and the Caribbean. These sea animals
were all selected for their adaptability to the

environment and compatibility with other species. Angelfish, puffer fish, tangs and other exotic sea creatures. One of the most elaborate and technically advanced aquariums in the world, the tank is 53 feet long, eight feet from top to bottom, and six feet from front to back. The acrylic used in the aquarium is 4 inches thick. The interior was carefully created to simulate an intricately detailed, coral reef. To preserve the living reefs in the ocean, no live coral is used in the tank.

ATOMIC TESTING MUSEUM
755 East Flamingo Rd., Las Vegas: 702-794-5151
http://nationalatomictestingmuseum.org/
The Atomic Testing Museum offers a permanent 8,000 sq. ft. gallery and the ATM Store, a specialty gift shop. Open Monday-Saturday 9-5 weekdays; Sundays 1-5. Closed Thanksgiving Day, Christmas Day and New Years Day. Admission fee.

BARRICK MUSEUM
4505 Maryland Pkwy., Las Vegas: 702-895-3011
http://barrickmuseum.unlv.edu
Outdoor xeriscape demonstration garden, live desert reptiles, mammals and insects, natural history and anthropology.

BELLAGIO CONSERVATORY & BOTANICAL GARDENS
3600 Las Vegas Blvd S., Las Vegas: 702-693-7111
http://www.bellagio.com/amenities/botanical-garden.aspx

To ensure the Conservatory & Botanical Gardens maintains magnificence 365 days a year, 140 expert horticulturists theatrically arrange gazebos, bridges, ponds, and water features uniquely for each season. Treat yourself to this unrivaled attraction's ever-changing personality.

BOULDER CITY / HOOVER DAM MUSEUM
Located in the Boulder Dam Hotel
1305 Arizona St., Boulder City: 702-294-1988
www.bchdmuseum.org
Free movie screening, "The Construction of Hoover Dam," and historical memorabilia relating to the workers and construction of Hoover Dam. Gift shop. Donation. Open 10-4.

BRUNO'S INDIAN MUSEUM
1306 Nevada Hwy., Boulder City: 702-293-4865
Bruno's Indian Museum promotes and educates the public about the Native American artists of the Southwest, of which 2,000 are represented in the fine art gallery and jewelry store. Daily 10-5.

CARROLL SHELBY MUSEUM
6405 Ensworth St., Las Vegas: 702-942-7325
http://www.shelby.com
See 35 years of Shelby performance cars and the company's 100,000 sq ft. manufacturing facility for the Shelby Cobras and the new Series 1. Open Monday thru Friday 8-5. Free tours are held daily at 10:30am and by appointment at 3:30pm. Shelby American is located at the entrance to the Las Vegas Motor Speedway.

CENTRAL NEVADA MUSEUM

1900 Logan Field Road, Tonopah, (209 miles northwest of Las Vegas): 702-482-9676
www.tonopahnevada.com
Dedicated to the history of Nye and Esmeralda Counties, the museum houses fascinating artifacts from the area's early days as a mining boom town. Seasonal hours.

CLARK COUNTY HERITAGE MUSEUM

1830 S. Boulder Hwy., Henderson: 702-455-7955
www.clarkcountynv.gov/depts/parks/pages/clark-county-museum.aspx
County history museum with exhibits, restored historic structures and ghost town.

DREAM RACING

Las Vegas Motor Speedway
7000 Las Vegas Blvd., N., Las Vegas: 702-605-3000
www.dreamracing.com
Ever dreamed of being a race car driver? Everybody has. Here's your big chance. After a short classroom lecture (about 15-minutes) that tells you how to actually handle yourself behind the wheel of a racecar, you'll experience a 3-D simulator that recreates what high-speed racing is really like. Then it's time to put on your helmet and get behind the wheel of a Ferrari F430 for your spin around the track. If you want the sensation of being in a racecar but are afraid to drive it, you can buy their Hot Laps package. A driver will take you around the track at speeds you've never been before.

EROTIC HERITAGE MUSEUM
3275 Sammy Davis Jr. Dr., Las Vegas: 702-794-4000
www.eroticmuseumvegas.com
Explore the vast array of socio-cultural perspectives
depicting erotic heritage, including a special emphasis
on the unfolding of the American Sexual Revolution
of the 20th Century. The Museum seeks to bridge the
gap between that which is commercial and often
misidentified as pornographic, with that which is
aesthetic, often identified as folk, pop, and fine art
through a common visual language.

FLAMINGO GARDEN LAS VEGAS
3555 Las Vegas Blvd S., Las Vegas: 702-733-3349
www.flamingolasvegas.com
A 15-acre garden with Flamingos and other exotic
birds, as well as koi and turtles.

FOUNTAIN SHOW@ BELLAGIO
3600 Las Vegas Blvd. S., Las Vegas: 702-693-7111
www.bellagio.com

A refreshing addition to your entertainment options, the Fountains of Bellagio were destined to romance your senses. Take in a free Las Vegas show of water, music and light thoughtfully interwoven to mesmerize its admirers.

GALLERY OF FINE ART @ BELLAGIO
3600 Las Vegas Blvd S., Las Vegas: 702-693-7871
http://www.bellagio.com/amenities/gallery-of-fine-art.aspx
BGFA is committed to presenting intimate exhibitions featuring works by some of the world's most compelling artists. BGFA exhibitions are organized in partnership with museums and foundations from around the world.

GALLERY OF HISTORY
3601 West Sahara Ave., Las Vegas: 702-364-1000
www.galleryofhistory.com
Historical documents framed as elegant works of art. Located in The Fashion Show Mall.

GEORGE L. STURMAN MUSEUM OF FINE ART
107 E Charleston Blvd., Las Vegas: 702-384-2615
The museum houses contemporary artwork from many famous artists such as Alexander Calder, Salvador Dali, Willem De Kooning, Robert De Niro, and Henri Matisse to name a few. In addition, an extensive collection of African art, animation cells and comic strip art, American art, Master Drawings and Paintings are also on display. 10:30-4 daily.

GOLDWELL OPEN AIR MUSEUM
West of Beatty, NV near Rhyolite: 702-870-9946
http://www.goldwellmuseum.org
The Goldwell Open Air Museum is a 15-acre outdoor
sculpture park approximately 5 miles west of the
town of Beatty and 120 miles north of Las Vegas. It is
a free admission facility, open year-round, 24 hours a
day, seven days a week. It began as a project of
Belgian artist Albert Szukalski in 1984 with the
installation of his major sculpture, "The Last Supper,"
which he created in cooperation with several Beatty
residents. In subsequent years, six additional pieces
were added to the site by three other Belgian artists
(Fred Bervoets, Hugo Heyrman, and Dre Peeters)
who, like Szukalski, were major figures in European
art with extensive exhibition records.

GONDOLA RIDE AT THE VENETIAN HOTEL
3355 Las Vegas Blvd, S., Las Vegas: 702-414-4300
www.venetian.com
Includes a visit to St. Mark's Square. Admission fee.

KAYAK ADVENTURES LAS VEGAS
1647-A Nevada Highway, Boulder City: 702-293-
5026
www.kayaklasvegas.com
Paddle the Colorado River from the base of Hoover
Dam to Willow Beach Arizona, hike to hot springs
from the river. Paddle to island beaches for a swim at
Lake Mead.

LAS VEGAS CHINATOWN PLAZA
4205 W. Spring Mountain Rd., Las Vegas: 702-221-8448
www.lvchinatownplaza.com/
About 1 mile west of Treasure Island, take a westbound CAT Route 203 bus from the intersection of Las Vegas Boulevard and Spring Mountain Road between TI and Fashion Show Mall. A place to experience Asian culture.

LAS VEGAS INDOOR SKY DIVING
200 Convention Center Dr., Las Vegas: 702-731-4768
www.vegasindoorskydiving.com
At 14,000 feet above Las Vegas, no one can hear your delighted screams... New skydivers start here.

LAS VEGAS NATURAL HISTORY MUSEUM
900 Las Vegas Blvd North, Las Vegas: 702-384-3466
http://www.lvnhm.org
Features animated dinosaurs, Southern Nevada's plant and animal life, international wildlife room, shark exhibit with live sharks, children's hands-on exploration room, and gift shop. Now open, a new floor to the Museum featuring exhibits about the African Savanna and African Rainforest. Also features Treasures of Egypt. Open Daily 9-4. Admission: Moderate fee

DISCOVERY CHILDREN'S MUSEUM
360 Promenade Pl., Las Vegas, 702-382-KIDS
www.discoverykidslv.org

Touch, see, explore, and experience over 100 hands-on science and art exhibits in one of the country's largest children's museums. Open Tuesday - Sunday 10am to 5pm and most school holidays. Admission: Small fee

LIGUORI'S ART & JEWELRY GALLERY-MUSEUM
567 Nevada Way, Boulder City: 702-293-4865
This art gallery-museum features sculpture and jewelry by native Las Vegan Steven Liguori, artwork and jewelry from various local artists, raw precious and semi-precious stones, and historical relics from the construction of the Hoover Dam. Local guest artists are featured here throughout the year. (Located on the corner of Nevada Way & Wyoming St. on the scenic route to Hoover Dam)

LOST CITY MUSEUM OF ARCHAEOLOGY
721 S. Moapa Valley Blvd, Overton: 702-397-2193
http://nvculture.org/lostcitymuseum/
Located 60 miles north of Las Vegas. Exhibits include artifacts of the Anasazi culture that colonized the Moapa Valley from the 1st to the 12th Century A.D. Reconstructed structures are on site. Open 8:30-4:30 Thursday – Sunday. Admission: Small fee

MACHINE GUNS VEGAS
3501 Aldebaran Ave., Las Vegas: 800-757-4668
www.machinegunsvegas.com
After you visit the **Mob Museum** (see listing below), you might be in the mood to shoot a few rounds yourself in this specialized shooting range offering 10

lanes. (They have 2 private lanes with a special entrance for VIPs who don't want the general public to see them.) This off-the-Strip place has hostesses that assist you in selecting your weapon of choice from an iPad display: how about an Uzi, or an M4 carbine or an AK-47? Women called "range masters" help you as you shoot and make sure you don't kill yourself or somebody else. Depending on your weapon of choice (and the ammo you use), Fees vary depending on weapon and ammo used. Free transport from The Strip. (You get a t-shirt and your targets as keepsakes.)

MCCARRAN AVIATION MUSEUM
McCarran International Airport
5757 Wayne Newton Blvd., Las Vegas: 702-261-5211
www.mccarran.com/
The Museum shows the history of aviation in Southern Nevada, from the first flight in 1920 through the introduction of jets. The Museum focuses on the history of commercial and general aviation, and is open 24 hours a day. The Museum's main exhibit is located above baggage claim on level two, with an additional exhibit in the general and corporate aviation terminal operated by Signature Flight Support. Free.

MOB MUSEUM
300 Stewart Ave., Las Vegas: 702-229-2734
www.themobmuseum.org
They spent $42 million on this place that glamorizes the American gangster. Don't you love it? (And it's

117

even located in an old courthouse.) More than you thought you wanted to know about characters such as Al Capone, John Gotti, Sam Giancana, Meyer Lansky, "Bugsy" Siegel, "Lucky" Luciano and Joe Bonanno. My favorite thing: the wall up against which all the victims were shot in the St. Valentine's Day Massacre. They brought the whole wall here. Exhibits detailing gangland figures, Tommy guns, undercover agents, wiretap equipment, interactive displays.

NEON MUSEUM
NEON BONEYARD
BONEYARD
The Fremont Street 'Galleries'
770 N Las Vegas Blvd, Las Vegas, 702-387-6366
www.neonmuseum.org
The Neon Museum officially "opened" with the installation of its first refurbished sign, The Hacienda Horse and Rider, on November 15, 1996, at the intersection of Las Vegas Boulevard and Fremont Street. Today some 200+ signs can be seen, seven of which have been restored. The campus covers 2 acres, includes an outdoor exhibition area, which opened in 2012. The visitors center is itself worth the trip—it's located in the preserved La Concha Motel lobby, a weird shell-shaped building that looks like a series of nuns' habits soaring into the sky.

NEVADA STATE MUSEUM AND HISTORICAL SOCIETY
309 S. Valley View Blvd., Las Vegas: 702-486-5205
www.nvculture.org/nevadastatemuseumlasvegas

A nationally accredited museum located in Lorenzi Park, presents Southern Nevada's history from mammoths to gambling. Galleries: Biology, Earth Science, History/Anthropology, Museum Store. Admission: Small fee. Open Daily 9-5.

PINBALL HALL OF FAME
1610 E Tropicana Ave, Las Vegas, 702-597-2627
www.pinballmuseum.org
NEIGHBORHOOD: University
ADMISSION: FREE
Since 2006, this place a couple of miles from the Strip has been attracting pinball fanatics from all over the globe. Many of the machines are one of a kind but unlike other museums they are all available for play – 10,000 square feet of pinball fun. Most of the employees are actually volunteers, they love the place so mch. It regularly ranks higher as an attraction than Stratosphere Tower, the Grand Canal Shoppes and the Neon Museum. Kids love this place. (So do arrested adolescents.) Vending machine offers bottled water, non-alcoholic beverages and ice cream. Open late.

SEARCHLIGHT MUSEUM
200 Michael Wendell Way, Searchlight: 702-297-1642
https://searchlightmuseum.org
The Searchlight Heritage Museum, a satellite of the Clark County Heritage Museum, reports the history of the mining boom town of Searchlight, which once surpassed Las Vegas in population. The story of Searchlight mining and railroad heritage and its many colorful pioneer citizens is told through photos,

artifacts, exhibits, and an outdoor mining park. The Museum is housed in the Community Center in Searchlight, 60 miles south of Las Vegas on Highway 65. Admission is free. Open Mon-Wed 1 to 5; Thursday, 1 to 9pm & Sat 9 to 1.

SHARK REEF AT MANDALAY BAY
3950 Las Vegas Boulevard S., Las Vegas: 702-632-4555
www.sharkreef.com
The Shark Reef at Mandalay Bay encompasses nearly 2 million gallons of water and reaches depths of 22 feet. One of the largest exhibits of its kind. The highlight is walking through a transparent tunnel with sharks, sea turtles, fishes of all kinds. ADMISSION: Moderate fee.

SHOOT AN AUTOMATIC WEAPON @ THE GUN STORE

2900 E Tropicana Ave., Las Vegas: 702- 454-1110
www.thegunstorelasvegas.com
The Gun Store has become one of Las Vegas' top places to visit, catering to tourists from all around the world and exhibiting a vast selection of firearms in both the retail store and shooting range.

SHOOT LAS VEGAS

South Las Vegas Blvd, Las Vegas, 702-634-4867
www.shootlasvegas.com
NEIGHBORHOOD: Southeast
A VIP shooting range experience located indoors. No dirt or heat, shooters stand in the comfort of a climate controlled firing line shooting at steel targets with more than 50 guns to select from. Choose anything from a Full Auto Machine Gun to a Sniper rifle. Shooting stations are equipped with photo/video systems that take your photo while you shoot. Shoot at multiple targets – including some that explode. You can even blow up a car. Variety of packages available with transportation included.

SIEGFRIED & ROY'S SECRET GARDEN AND DOLPHIN HABITAT

3400 Las Vegas Boulevard S., Las Vegas: 702-791-7188
http://www.mirage.com/attractions/secret-garden.aspx
This may end up being your favorite "attraction" in Vegas. Here you can really "play with the dolphins." The staff here are always punching big beach balls

out over the water. The dolphins jump up and bounce them right back. And you can participate. (You might get a little damp, but it's as thrilling for a jaded grown-up as it is for a 10-year-old child.) This is not some oh-by-the-way operation, either, in the way "alligator wrestling" farms are in the Florida Everglades. This is a highly sophisticated affair. Here, you have three large pools of saltwater (they make the salt water here and filter it every two hours). The viewing ports are varied and you can see the animals from different perspectives, from above or from below. (Try all of them; each perspective is a thrill.)

SUN BUGGY
6925 Speedway Boulevard, Las Vegas: 866-728-4443
www.sunbuggy.com/lasvegas
Dune buggy rentals and off-roading experiences at the Las Vegas dunes.

THE TANK @ GOLDEN NUGGET
129 E. Fremont St. Las Vegas: 702-385-7111
www.goldennugget.com/
A $30 million complex complete with a shark tank, a 3-story waterslide and 17 private cabanas.

THUNDERBIRD MUSEUM

4445 Tyndall Ave., Nellis Air Force Base: 702-652-6776 (call to confirm they're open)
afthunderbirds.com/site/
The Thunderbirds offer public tours of their facility every Tuesday and Thursday at 2pm. The tour is not held on federal holidays or during the team's Christmas, Easter and mid-season break. To attend the tour, people must be at the Nellis AFB Main Gate (located on Las Vegas Boulevard at the intersection of Craig Rd. by 1:45pm. There you get a visitor's pass that gives you access to the base. You need a driver's license, current registration and proof of insurance for your vehicle. For rental vehicles, a drivers license and a copy of the rental contract is sufficient. Please note that no transportation is provided from the Main Gate to the Thunderbird Hangar. The tour includes a short video, guided museum walk-through and a chance to look at a Thunderbird F-16 up close (depending on aircraft availability).

TOILETS @ MAIN STREET STATION

200 N. Main St., Las Vegas: 702-387-1896
http://www.mainstreetcasino.com
The urinals in the men's room are mounted on a piece of the Berlin Wall. If you're one of the fairer sex, ask an employee to let you see it, they almost always will accommodate you.

U.S. ROUTE 95 AT NIGHT

This route climbs gradually northwest of Las Vegas so that The Strip's lights remain visible for a remarkably long distance, appearing as a luminous cloud from the furthest point.

VOLCANO AT THE MIRAGE
3400 Las Vegas Boulevard S., Las Vegas: 702-791-7111
www.mirage.com/en/amenities/volcano.html
Known the world over for its iconic feature on The Strip, the Mirage has joined forces with legendary Grateful Dead drummer Mickey Hart, Indian tabla sensation Zakir Hussain and Fountains of Bellagio design firm WET to create an all-new audio/visual spectacle.

WALKER AFRICAN-AMERICAN MUSEUM
705 W. Van Buren, Las Vegas: 702-752-647-2242
Preserves and promotes the history of people of African descent. The museum offers over 10,000 items consisting of ethnic dolls, art, artifacts, figurines, posters, prints, books, magazines, buttons, records, and personal items of renowned African-Americans and much more. The museum's gift shop offers an array of Afrocentric art, gifts, greeting cards, fashion and accessories. The museum also publishes "Black Pioneers of Nevada," which highlights the accomplishments of Pioneers past and present. This is the only annual publication of its kind.

WORLD'S LARGEST GOLDEN NUGGET
129 East Fremont St., Las Vegas: 702-385-7111
http://www.goldennugget.com

In Downtown Las Vegas, you can see up close the largest golden nugget in the world at the Golden Nugget Las Vegas Hotel. The exhibit is open for viewing 24 hours a day.

FREE THINGS TO DO

AQUARIUM AT THE SILVERTON HOTEL
SILVERTON
3333 Blue Diamond Rd., Las Vegas: 702-263-7777
http://www.silvertoncasino.com
Your eyes aren't fooling you if you happen to see a mermaid floating through the aquarium at the Silverton Casino Lodge.
Throughout the afternoon and evenings Thursday through Sunday, women dressed as mermaids join the 4,000 tropical fish, including three species of stingrays and three species of sharks, in the 117,000-gallon, curved acrylic tank, for a 15-minute show. While hotel guests are entertained and amazed, the fish, themselves, remain fairly aloof.
"The fish don't seem to care one way or the other that we're in there," said Timery Middelton, a mermaid at the Silverton. "We're just another object in the water and they pretty much stay out of our way. There are some fish that are curious because our costumes are bright and shiny and that's very appealing. But for the most part they know us and go on their way."

BARRICK MUSEUM
4505 S. Maryland Pkwy., Las Vegas: 702-895-3381

http://barrickmuseum.unlv.edu

For more than 40 years, the University of Nevada Las Vegas' Marjorie Barrick Museum has been a cultural gathering place for UNLV students, faculty, staff, and alumni; the Las Vegas Community; and visitors alike. The museum hosts a rotating series of exhibitions featuring modern and contemporary art, as well as, a stunning collection of pre-Hispanic Mesoamerican ceramics, Mexican dance masks, and Southwestern native crafts. We encourage you to explore the exhibits, attend an event, meet friends or have lunch in the garden.

BELLAGIO CONSERVATORY & BOTANICAL GARDENS

3600 Las Vegas Blvd. S., Las Vegas: 702-693-7111

http://www.bellagio.com

Brilliance abounds inside their breathtaking Conservatory & Botanical Gardens. The attention to detail is astounding. The passionate display of nature in all its awe-evoking glory - quite simply, sensational.

Admire the essence of every season recreated with exceptionally gorgeous plants, flowers and trees thoughtfully arranged. Specially designed lighting spotlights every flower to accentuate its best features. To ensure the Conservatory & Botanical Gardens maintains magnificence 365 days a year, 140 expert horticulturists theatrically arrange gazebos, bridges, ponds, and water features uniquely for each season.

CBS TELEVISION CITY RESEARCH CENTER
MGM GRAND
3799 S. Las Vegas Blvd., Las Vegas: 702-891-5753
www.tvcityresearch.com
Ever thought you could do the job of a network
executive, deciding which shows are put on the air
and which ones end up in the waste bin?
Network jobs are hard to come by, but you can weigh
in on the decision-making process by letting your
opinions be known at the CBS Television City
Research Center at MGM Grand.
You could find a gem, such as the pilot to a great new
series -- or you could get a rip-off of a current show
(we won't name names here). Half the fun, though, is
the anticipation.

Participation is quite effortless. Viewers can pick up
tickets in front of the research center. They then
register at the counter in front of the center and line
up about 10 minutes before their scheduled time.

Five minutes before the screening begins, viewers are
led into one of four studios to watch the latest
offerings from CBS, MTV, Nickelodeon and other
Viacom networks (the television-holdings giant
manages the research center).

Viewers then are instructed on how to use the test
pads and monitors to register their opinions, and settle
into the viewing process.

The show's length will determine the time of the
testing process. A survey following the program lasts

about 15 minutes, so viewers should expect an hour for an hour-long show (actually 45 minutes, as it is shown with no commercials). And since everything is done through touch screen, you won't have to worry about your hand cramping up from writing.

The attraction also offers testing for commercials, websites and technology-based products. Products tested in the past include Nintendo Wii, Xbox 360, Apple iPhone and Dell notebook computers.

ETHEL M CHOCOLATES
2 Cactus Garden Drive, Henderson: 702-435-2608
http://www.ethelm.com
For an all-out chocolate experience, visitors must check out the Ethel M Chocolate Factory and Botanical Cactus Gardens, which also includes an Ethel's lounge.
Located in Henderson, Ethel M Chocolate Factory and Cactus Gardens is quite the adventure. Only 15 minutes away from The Strip, it attracts more than 700,000 tourists a year. Guests get to see chocolates being made, sample gourmet treats and meander through the maze of paths at the Botanical Cactus Gardens at no charge.
"Our chocolate factory and cactus garden provides a non-traditional tourist attraction for visitors to Las Vegas, a good alternative to the standard Las Vegas Strip," said John Haugh, president of Mars Retail Group.
Picking up a piece of chocolate and popping it in your mouth only takes a second. Preparing the filling, texture and shape of it takes a lot longer. At the Ethel

M Chocolate Factory, visitors witness the time and effort it takes to create that perfect morsel.

In fact, this factory has a series of pipes, conveyer belts and tanks that hold 20,000 and 35,000 gallons of chocolate.

EIFFEL TOWER RESTAURANT AT PARIS HOTEL
3655 Las Vegas Boulevard S., Las Vegas: 702-948-6937
www.parislasvegas.com
The Eiffel Tower restaurant is located on the 11th floor of the Eiffel Tower replica at Paris. Guests are whisked up to the restaurant level by an all-glass elevator located inside the scenic Paris casino. Once you step inside the romantic, dimly lit restaurant you will find a stunning panoramic view of the Las Vegas Strip. This is an upscale experience (no shorts allowed) but even if you can't fit a full dinner into the budget, take 30 minutes from your evening and sit at

the bar and have one drink. It is, by far, the best
vantage point to watch the Bellagio fountains.

FORUM SHOPS FOUNTAIN SHOWS
CAESARS PALACE
3500 Las Vegas Blvd. S., Las Vegas: 702-893-4800
http://www.caesarspalace.com
Just when you thought you had seen it all, the Fall of
Atlantis Fountain Show will captivate you with its
stunning special effects. Located in the Forum Shops,
next to The Cheesecake Factory, the free fountain
show uses lifelike animatronic figures to recount the
myth of Atlantis.
The story unfolds as King Atlas tries to determine
which of his children will rule Atlantis. The siblings
try to destroy each another, poisoning the kingdom
with their greed. Finally, the gods decide to step in
and settle the dispute, launching the Fall of Atlantis.
A 20-foot winged beast appears from behind Atlas'
throne and watches over the destruction as Atlantis is
consumed by fire and then flooding water.
Surrounding monitors add to the drama of the show
with a variety of visual displays. Be sure to get to the
show a few minutes early to grab a good spot; the
area gets crowded quickly.
Once the show concludes, take a walk behind the
fountain and check out more than 100 species of
ocean life in a 50,000-gallon saltwater aquarium.
You can watch as a diver feeds the tropical puffers,
flounder, sharks and the rest of the aquarium's
inhabitants each day at 1:15 and 5:15 pm. A second
staff person is present during feeding times to answer
any questions you might have. In addition, tours of

the aquarium's facilities are offered Monday through Friday at 3:15 p.m.

FOUNTAINS OF BELLAGIO
Bellagio
3600 Las Vegas Blvd. S., Las Vegas: 702-693-7111
http://www.bellagio.com
A refreshing addition to your entertainment options, the Fountains of Bellagio were destined to romance your senses. Take in a free Las Vegas show of water, music and light thoughtfully interwoven to mesmerize its admirers. All for your amusement, the most ambitious, choreographically complex water feature ever conceived amazes against the beautiful backdrop of Las Vegas' lavender sky. Each dynamic performance from the Fountains collection is unique in its expression and interpretation. Fall in love with the stunning nature of this unprecedented aquatic accomplishment while relishing a clever concert of opera, classical and Broadway tunes.

FREMONT STREET EXPERIENCE
Fremont St., Las Vegas: 702-678-5600
www.vegasexperience.com
Welcome to Glitter Gulch. Located in Downtown Las Vegas, the Fremont Street Experience offers free nightly shows featuring 12.5 million lights and 550,000 watts of amazing sound. The show is often paired with free concerts and other special events. It's a modern twist on old-school Vegas. The show starts every hour on the hour from 7 pm. to midnight. On the east end of the street, walk through the outdoor

Neon Museum, which hosts some of the old hotels' neon signs.

SUNSET STAMPEDE AT SAM'S TOWN
SAM'S TOWN
5111 Boulder Hwy., Las Vegas: 702-456-7777
http://www.samstownlv.com
Similar to an old Western, the Sunset Stampede transports visitors back in time through the use of water, lasers, lights and animation.
The eight-minute show begins with the plaintive howl of an animatronic wolf, which suddenly appears at the top of the mountain. The wolf is joined by other wildlife, including a bear and an eagle.
The fountains come alive, shooting up to eight stories high and dancing along to a symphonic score recorded especially for Sam's Town by the Indianapolis Philharmonic Orchestra. The show chronicles the Western pioneer experience.
Sunset Stampede is located in Mystic Falls Park, a 25,000-square-foot live forest within an atrium. There is plenty of room for viewing the show, although those standing up front are likely to get a bit wet. A bar situated in the middle of the park provides a good vantage point while offering onlookers the chance to stay dry.
Once the show concludes, Mystic Falls becomes peaceful once more. Filled with lush foliage, cascading waterfalls and a babbling brook, the spot is the ideal location for relaxation. Wooden benches are scattered throughout the park, providing a place to sit and take in the view. And for those interested in a

leisurely stroll, stone walkways lined with rustic hanging lanterns weave their way through the park.

THE MIRAGE VOLCANO
The Mirage
3400 S. Las Vegas Blvd., Las Vegas: 702-791-7111
http://mirage.com
Known the world over for its iconic Strip-front feature, The Mirage has joined forces with legendary Grateful Dead drummer Mickey Hart, Indian tabla sensation Zakir Hussain and Fountains of Bellagio design firm WET to create an all-new audio/visual spectacle.

WILDLIFE HABITAT AT THE FLAMINGO
FLAMINGO
3555 S. Las Vegas Blvd., Las Vegas: 702-733-3349
http://www.flamingolasvegas.com
Amid the neon lights and slot machines, the Flamingo offers a refreshing oasis with its Wildlife Habitat. Guests will feel as if they have been transported to a tropical island as they take refuge in the habitat, located next to the Flamingo's pool area.
Full of photo opportunities, the habitat is filled with lush foliage imported from around the world including varieties of pines, palms and magnolia. Visitors can take a stroll on winding walkways alongside streams and waterfalls, or on bridges over lagoons and ponds. Benches scattered throughout the area allow guests the chance to sit back and enjoy the view.
The Wildlife Habitat at the Flamingo is home to more than 300 birds, including Impeyn and silver

pheasants, Gambel's quail, a Crown crane, two ibis, swans, ducks and parrots. However, the most notable are likely the Chilean flamingos.

But birds aren't the only wildlife that can be seen in the habitat; there is an abundance of turtles and koi as well.

WYNN CONSERVATORY

Wynn Las Vegas

3131 Las Vegas Boulevard S., Las Vegas: 702-770-7000

www.wynnlasvegas.com

Sure, you may not be into floral displays, but this won't take long to see and it is indeed a thing of beauty. The conservatory is conveniently located just inside the main entrance of Wynn Las Vegas so it's not like you have to search and find it. It's open 24 hours – although its exquisiteness is accentuated during the day as the sun shines down – and the display changes on a regular basis.

'WELCOME TO LAS VEGAS' SIGN

In the median at 5100 Las Vegas Boulevard South

Much like the famous "Hollywood" sign that sits in the hills of Los Angeles, the "Welcome to Las Vegas" sign is a world-famous landmark that you have seen hundreds of times online, in magazines or on TV. So while you're in town, why not seek it out and get a picture of everyone in your group standing there like dorks in front of it

WYNN LAKE OF DREAMS
WYNN HOTEL
3131 Las Vegas Blvd S., Las Vegas: 702-770-7000
http://www.wynnlasvegas.com
Experience the mystery of the Lake of Dreams at
Wynn Las Vegas. This secluded 3-acre lake is
surrounded by a lush forest and takes you away from
the chaos and noise of the city. Enjoy the water and
light show from various points around the lake
including several restaurants and lounges. Free
vantage points are also strategically located for
optimal viewing. The shows begin at 8:30 and occur
approximately every half hour until 1am daily. This is
a free attraction.

LAS VEGAS
FOR THE KIDS

In precisely the same way that Disneyworld is not just
for kids, Las Vegas is not just for adults. (Well…)

Truly, there are plenty of things to do away from the smoke, the sound of slots incessantly ringing in your ears and the hollers of joy (or groans of agony) rising from the frenetic group around the craps table.

First, check out **Chapter 6 – Attractions,** for a lot of different ideas for the kids. Below are some items more specifically suited to the kids not covered in that chapter.

CIRCUS CIRCUS HOTEL & CASINO

2880 Las Vegas Blvd S., Las Vegas: 702-734-0410
www.circuscircus.com
This long-time family-friendly hotel has oodles of stuff to keep the kids busy. I mean, oodles. They offer some 300 pinball and arcade-type video games for the kids (you'll find a lot of grownups here, too). Plus, there is an actual circus that runs, continuously, from 11 in the morning till midnight. So anytime of day you can slip in here and get the full treatment. And it's not your cheapskate circus. It's the real deal: stunt cyclists, high-wire acts, acrobats, jugglers, trapeze experts, clowns, magicians, you name it. There's a free aerial shuttle kids like to ride that makes getting around the Circus Circus complex a breeze.

ETHEL M CHOCOLATES

2 Cactus Garden Dr., Henderson: 800-438-4356
http://www.ethelm.com
 Free. A good idea if you have kids. (Or if you just like chocolate.) They have a self-guided tour that lets you breeze through the confectionary. Great demonstrations of candy-making techniques behind

glass walls. Takes you to their shop where you can sample any of the varieties you just saw being made. Here you can buy your favorites. Kids will love it as they watch how their favorite chocolate candy is made. Also has an expansive cactus garden if you have any interest in things botanical.

EXCALIBUR HOTEL & CASINO
3850 Las Vegas Blvd. S., Las Vegas: 702-597-7777
http://www.excalibur.com
This is another family-friendly hotel with lots of exciting things for kids. They have a running carnival with a Midway feeling. A virtual reality ride with the SpongeBob SquarePants theme is still packin' 'em in.

MADAME TUSSAUD'S WAX MUSEUM AT VENETIAN
3377 Las Vegas Blvd. S., Las Vegas: 702-862-7800
www.madametussauds.com/las-vegas/en/
Guests are allowed to touch and take photos of the wax figures and some of the figures will even react when people get close. This is a lot of fun and a great way to spend time with family in the wax museum. Variety of packages available.

NEW YORK NEW YORK ROLLER COASTER
3790 Las Vegas Blvd. S., Las Vegas: 702-740-6969
http://www.newyorknewyork.com
Located on the popular intersection of Tropicana Ave. and Las Vegas Blvd., The Roller Coaster at New York – New York is hard to miss. Set in a perfect postcard shot, its surroundings include a replica of the New York harbor, a 150-foot model of the Statue of

Liberty as well as several of Manhattan's popular buildings. And to make things even more fun, the roller coaster trains are designed like New York taxicabs making it one of the adventurous things to do in Las Vegas with kids.

SHARK REEF AQUARIUM AT MANDALAY BAY
3950 Las Vegas Blvd. S., Las Vegas: 702-632-4555
http://www.mandalaybay.com
The Shark Reef is home to more than 1,200 different species of sharks, tropical and fresh water fish, reptiles, marine invertebrates and rays. Lot of fun with family and visiting the Shark Reef Aquarium at Mandalay Bay is one of the awesome fun things to do in Las Vegas with kids. Sharks including blacktip reef sharks, whitetip reef sharks, bonnethead sharks, nurse sharks, sand tiger sharks, sandbar sharks, zebra sharks, white spotted bamboo sharks, port jackson sharks and lemon sharks. Tickets moderately priced.

STRATOSPHERE TOWER
2000 Las Vegas Blvd. S., Las Vegas: 800-99-TOWER
www.stratospherehotel.com
Famous rides like the Big Shot, Insanity and X Scream. The rides are really scary and it is only for older kids - at least 4 years old. If these rides seem too intense, there's no need to miss out on all the fun. Visitors can still watch their adventurous friends on the rides from the huge indoor Tower rising 1,100 feet. (It's the tallest freestanding observation deck in the U.S.)

V: THE ULTIMATE VARIETY SHOW AT PLANET HOLLYWOOD
3663 Las Vegas Blvd. S., Las Vegas: 702-932-1818
www.planethollywoodresort.com
This show is fun for families and gives the most bang for your buck. Your kids will love it since it includes magic, special effects, death-defying stunts, wild comedy, visual artists, physical insanity and much more.

GOLF COURSES

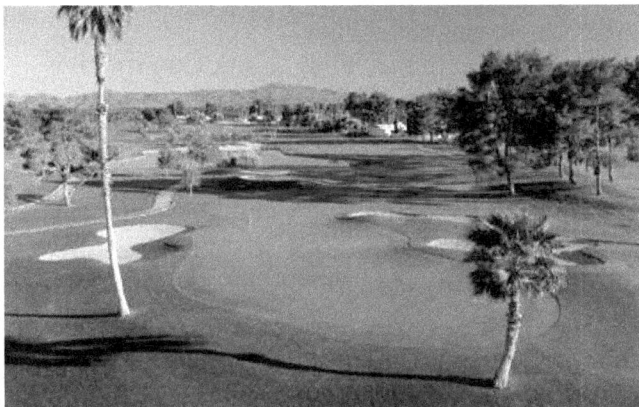

LAS VEGAS NATIONAL GOLF CLUB
1911 E Desert Inn Rd., Las Vegas: 702-889-1000
http://www.lasvegasnational.com
Play on 150 acres of grass. Whether you top it off the tee, yank it left, hit it right, or send it down the middle, you are playing on grass. The only rocks to contend with at Las Vegas National are in the

clubhouse bar, in a cocktail glass. One of the keys to fun golf is a reasonable pace of play. No six-hour rounds of golf at LVN.

THE LAS VEGAS COUNTRY CLUB
3000 Joe W. Brown Drive, Las Vegas: 702-734-1122
http://www.lasvegascc.com
The club is a place where business professionals meet, families celebrate and golfers enjoy the world class course. Recently re-opened the course after an 8 month, $5.4 million renovation. Been here for over 40 years.

LAS VEGAS GOLF CLUB
4300 W. Washington Ave., Las Vegas: 702-646-3003
http://www.lasvegasgc.com
The oldest course in the valley, Clark County's Las Vegas Golf Club (est. 1938) presents the quintessential player-friendly golf experience, but with something new: $5 million in recent improvements, including a new clubhouse and course upgrades. Several mature cottonwood and pine trees stand sparsely along the virtually bunker-less fairways. Thirty greenside bunkers add a degree of challenge, but the greens also are pretty accessible, with generally slight degrees of undulation. This is a perfect course for a relaxing, forgiving round. The first three holes offer a great chance to come out scoring. The first is a drivable, 311-yard par 4 with three bunkers long and right of the green. The second hole is the longest on the course: a 503-yard, slight dogleg-left par 5. Some trees guard the turn, but the fairway is wide while the green is guarded by a single

bunker left. The third hole, a 98-yard par 3 is the course's shortest, but it demands a solid wedge shot. The kidney-shaped green is fronted by a pond and backed by four bunkers.

BALI HAI GOLF CLUB
5160 Las Vegas Blvd. S., Las Vegas: 866-330-5178
http://www.balihaigolfclub.com
Treat yourself and your game to the Bali Hai Golf Club. You deserve it. This is the Las Vegas Golf Club that transports you from the hustle and bustle of the casino floor, to 7,002 yards of tropical golfer's paradise. Within seconds of entering the property, yet with the skyline of The Strip still in sight, you will feel the mood and scenery change into the tranquility and beauty of a south pacific resort.

RHODES RANCH GOLF CLUB
20 Rhodes Ranch Parkway, Las Vegas: 702-740-4114
http://www.rhodesranchgolf.com
Located just a few minutes from The Strip. Built by legendary architect Ted Robinson. The layout presents a one of a kind mixture of challenge and playability for golfers of all talent levels. Highlighted by a collection of par 3's which Robinson calls the very finest that he has ever designed. This 6,909-yard course features a rich tropical environment as well as a world-class golf experience.

Chapter 7
EXCURSIONS

THE GRAND CANYON
928-638-7888 / www.nps.gov/grca

The Grand Canyon is one of the most popular excursions from Las Vegas, and there are almost as many activity options as there are people willing to take you there. For many, this will be the highlight of their stay, so it pays to do a bit of pre-trip research to ensure you make the most of your time.

If you're not planning to make your own way there, you can reach the canyon by small plane (with raised wings for excellent viewing), helicopter or bus, though it's also possible to go by Hummer (a rugged terrain vehicle) or even by boat or raft for part of the way.

One of the more recent attractions is the Skywalk, managed by the Hualapai Tribe. Located on the West Rim's tribal lands, it's a glass-bottomed structure, which projects about 70 feet out over the canyon's rim and allows you to gaze down 4,000 feet to the Colorado River below. (You go first. I tried, but couldn't do it.)

THE HOOVER DAM
702-494-2517
www.usbr.gov/lc/hooverdam
Straddling the border between Nevada and Arizona, the Hoover Dam was completed in 1936 and along with the Panama Canal and Brooklyn Bridge is often proclaimed to be one of the seven technical wonders of the world.

Lying just 30 miles southeast of Las Vegas, the Hoover Dam and Lake Mead (the reservoir created by the dam's construction) are often visited as part of a trip to the Grand Canyon, but there's easily enough to see and do here to warrant a full day's visit.

As with the Grand Canyon, the Hoover Dam can be reached by road or air, with tours by helicopter being especially popular as they can fly at lower altitudes, for a genuinely thrilling aerial view. (To fully appreciate what a masterpiece of engineering this is, you really do need to see it from the air.)

LAKE LAS VEGAS

Created as a playground for the rich and famous (Céline Dion has a house here), Lake Las Vegas is a man-made reservoir created in a formerly dry, dusty valley about 20 miles east of the city on the way to Lake Mead. Surrounded by multimillion-dollar houses and rambling upscale condominium complexes, the bulk of the area is privately owned; but curving gracefully around the western lip of the lake is MonteLago Village, an homage to an Italian seaside community featuring accommodations, dining, shopping, entertainment, recreation, and even gambling options for those with a taste (and a budget) for the finer things in life.

LAKE MEAD

702-293-8990

The manmade "lake" came into being when the Hoover Dam went up in 1936, stopping the Colorado River. It covers over 2,300 square miles. In addition to providing the water that feeds those fountains at the Bellagio, the Lake Mead National Recreation Area is a resource attracting almost 10 million visitors who explore, fish, rent boats, picnic, camp, swim and everything else you can do in or on the water.

MT. CHARLESTON

702-872-5486

www.gomtcharleston.com

Mt. Charleston is 35 miles (56 kilometers) from Las Vegas with its highest elevation at 11,918 feet (3,615 meters). An average of 20 to 30 degrees cooler than Las Vegas, Mt. Charleston is perfect for skiing,

picnicking, hiking and horseback riding. In addition
to year-round lodgings and tours, full-service
camping is also available from May through
September. This is not your typical Las Vegas
experience.

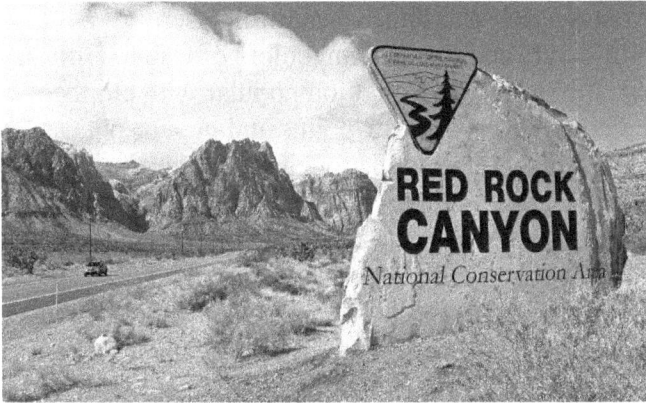

RED ROCK CANYON
702-515-5350
www.redrockcanyonlv.org
For the more adventurous traveller, a trip to the
dramatic red rock formations and sandstone peaks of
Red Rock Canyon National Conservation Area is a
must. Only 17 miles west of Las Vegas, it's an easily
accessible side-trip, though you'll feel like you're a
world away from the lights and chaos of The Strip
(despite the canyon being clearly visible from many
of The Strip's high vantage points).
The canyon was granted National Conservation Area
status in 1990, recognizing the unique geology and
wildlife of its surroundings, though it's
predominantly the excellent hiking, mountain biking

and rock-climbing opportunities that entice the 1 million visitors who come here each year.

A good way to get your bearings is to drive (either in a hired car or as part of a tour) the 13-mile scenic drive, which offers panoramic views of the spectacular desert landscape. Along the way you'll see fossilized sand dunes, beautiful desert wildflowers and the brilliant colors of Calico Hills, a majestic sandstone formation popular with climbers. There are numerous viewpoints and picnic spots as well as the obligatory visitor center, which houses a desert tortoise habitat.

To really feel the spirit of the canyon though, you'll need to get out and walk. There are trails for all fitness levels, starting with an easy 0.7 mile loop to the waterfall at Lost Creek through to much more strenuous treks such as the 11 mile Grand Circle Adventure. Remember to watch your footing on the loose rocks and keep a lookout for snakes. If you prefer a guided hike, check out local company Hike This.

ST. GEORGE, UT

St. George, Utah, is a year round recreational haven less than a two-hour drive away from Las Vegas on Interstate 15. Like Las Vegas, St. George enjoys hot summers and mild winters. The city is known for its outlet shopping, year round golf courses, two theater companies that bring Broadway to the desert, and great recreational facilities. October is a great time of year to visit the city since the St. George Marathon - one of the best marathons to build a vacation around according to Runner's World Magazine - and the

Huntsman World Senior Games, which attracts thousands of athletes (50 years and older) to compete in many sports.

Chapter 8
GAY LAS VEGAS

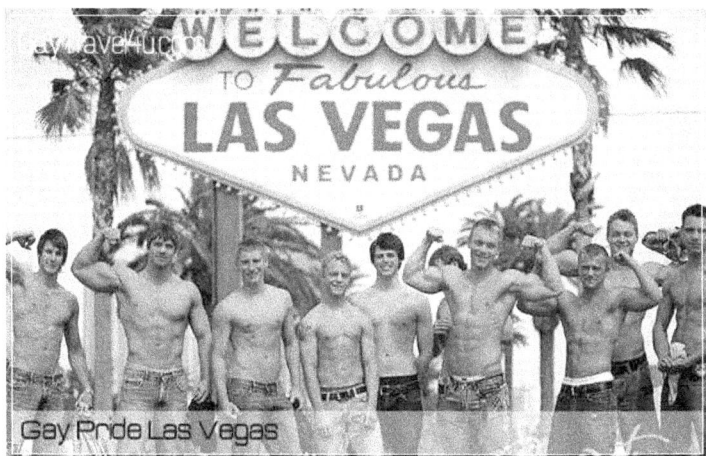

Gay Pride Las Vegas

BADLANDS SALOON
Commercial Center - 953 E. Sahara Ave., Las Vegas: 702-792-9262
https://badlandsbarlv.com
Neighborhood country/western bar. You'll feel like you've walked into the Wild West in this friendly neighborhood bar. The jukebox is very country and the regulars are really regular (they even keep their own beer mugs here).

CHARLIE'S
5012 Arville St., Las Vegas: 702-876-1844
http://www.charlieslasvegas.com
Popular country & western dance bar. Part of the
Charlie's chain, this club features drink specials and
live DJs Wednesday through Sunday and line dancing
lessons on Thursdays from 7-9 p.m. Sunday afternoon
beer blasts pack them in starting around 4 pm.
Wednesday, $2 well drinks for guys who show off in
their underwear.

FUN HOG RANCH
495 E. Twain Ave., Las Vegas: 702-791-7001
http://www.funhogranchlv.com
The Fun Hog Ranch attracts patrons with a casual and
festive atmosphere. The ranch's unique central Las
Vegas location (just off Paradise on Twain) makes it
easily accessible to the entire city and surrounding
suburbs.
Being highly accessible, men will easily find a
comfortable place to hang out, drink and make new
friends. The friendly staff is always available to fix
you a drink and they're just plain fun to look at. Don't
be afraid to be yourself at FHR. Exposed wood,
booths and a rustic atmosphere provides for a laid
back attitude. Fetish wear/leather is strongly
encouraged and street wear can be sexy and fun also.

FREEZONE
Paradise Fruit Loop - 610 E. Naples Dr., Las Vegas:
702-794-2300
http://www.freezonelv.com

FREEZONE is the premier alternative nightclub for tourists and locals of Las Vegas. It has been featured in national magazines and numerous websites and is centrally located to the Hard Rock Hotel, UNLV, and the famous Las Vegas Strip. This 24/7 Nightclub has been thriving for the past 10 years with laser lights flashing, liquor flowing from the hands of the gorgeous and friendly staff, beautiful people dancing to the most recent tunes whether it be on the dance pole or on the spacious dance floor. FREEZONE features QUEENS OF LAS VEGAS, the longest running drag show in Las Vegas with world renowned Shawn M. Patrons enjoy video gaming machines, pool tables, arcade games, with daily happy hour and Friday martini social all along with restaurant to fulfill dining pleasures.

LAS VEGAS EAGLE
3430 E. Tropicana Ave., Las Vegas: 702-458-8662
Leather and Levis at this Vegas outpost. Off the beaten track, but in a good way, this place is a welcome relief from the intensity and self-consciousness of the bigger Vegas bars. Wednesdays and Fridays: Get a free drink for stripping down to boxers or briefs. Where else do you get free stuff for getting naked?

PIRANHA NIGHTCLUB
Paradise Fruit Loop - 4633 Paradise Rd., Las Vegas: 702-791-0100
http://www.piranhavegas.com
Designed as a mansion with old world charm, the club embraces guests in a world of decadent

opulence. Enjoy dancing in the lounge, or take in the scenery of the main ballroom dance floor featuring the best local and world renowned DJs. Las Vegas' Only Gay Boutique Nightclub located in the heart of Gay Las Vegas' Fruit Loop. Doors open nightly at 10pm, 7 Nights a week.

INDEX

153

www.ingramcontent.com/pod-product-compliance
Lightning Source LLC
Chambersburg PA
CBHW060831050426

42453CB00008B/655